From Ethiopia
to Utopia

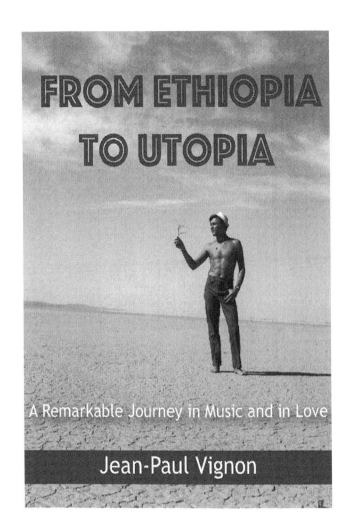

FROM ETHIOPIA TO UTOPIA

A Remarkable Journey in Music and in Love

Jean-Paul Vignon

Côte d'Azur 🌴 Californie

FROM ETHIOPIA TO UTOPIA
A Remarkable Journey in Music and in Love

ISBN 978-0-692-06473-3

CONTENTS

INTRODUCTION

I AM NOT a movie star, I am not a rock star, and I have not sold millions of records... but I *have* had my fifteen minutes!

I am not a scientist, and I certainly don't know how to do a heart transplant—even though, to please my father, I studied one year of medicine. But physics, chemistry and biology could not find their niche in my brain!

I am not a Republican, and I am not a Democrat; I am a very independent guy who asks questions and seeks the truth. I have learned not to trust any politician, whether or not they have written a book. I feel the same about religion.

I am not gay, though I admit to having some feminine traits. My favorite movie is "An Affair To Remember"; I proudly own a DVD of it. At the end, when Cary Grant says: "If it had to happen to one of us, why did it have to happen to you?" and Deborah Kerr responds: "Don't worry darling, if you can paint I can walk!"—I cry every time!

I did not invent anything, even though what I do to keep my hair is my own secret!

I am a complete moron when it comes to making money. But I am glad I never learned how to get the obscene amount of of dollars that CEOs receive when they are fired!

In this memoir, I have, of course, changed some names to protect the privacy of the characters who appeared in my life. I kept the real names of those who gave me their permission.

But, even though I have worked and played with some very famous people, their names mean less than the story in which they appear.

What makes a person interesting is not just success, influence or money. The intricacies of life and how one deals with them are the truly fascinating elements in any biography. So, when people ask me why I'd like to write the story of my life (since the public only buy books written by well known people), I simply reply: "Why not? After all, a man's journey from Ethiopia to Hollywood is *not* an everyday journey!"

CHAPTER 1

The Kingdom of Sheba

THEY FELL from the sky and bounced on the ground, like millions of pearls. The sky was painted grey that morning; even though it was January, this was a rare occurrence in that part of the world; the lower region of Ethiopia is near the equator, and the climate is tropical. It does not rain often... but when it does, it gives you an idea of what the Great Deluge was about! The little pearls of rain were leaping from the large leaves of the banana trees, to the papaya trees, to the mango trees, and every other leaf of exotic vegetation. They were laughing, screaming, jumping... and completely unaware that in the little clinic near by, a young lady was giving birth to a new baby.

The Bible and some scholars say The Kingdom of Sheba spread from the southern tip of Arabia, known today as Yemen, to the western shores of the Red Sea, including the fertile plains and mountains where the legendary river Nile has its source. The Kingdom of Sheba or Saba (meaning Host of Heaven) was rich in gold, precious stones, incense and exotic spices. It traded with its neighboring countries in camel caravans that traveled along the Red Sea, all the way to the Middle East.

The fabled female ruler of that country was the Queen of Sheba. The legend says that she was very beautiful and adventurous, and she became fascinated by a story one of her caravan guides told her about the wisdom of a great king who ruled the country called Israel. She was very curious, and willing to learn as much as she could about everything. She decided to travel by caravan to Jerusalem, to meet the wise king named Solomon. When they met, King Solomon fell madly in love with Sheba. Their affair was said to have created a special class of people who returned to the Kingdom of Sheba, where they developed an enlightened country that, long after the death of the Queen, was re-named Abyssinia. Through the centuries, Abyssinia became a self-sufficient country; the only country in black Africa with a grammar and a written language. The alphabetic characters of that language, Amharic, look very much like the characters of the Hebrew language, and is still used in the same country, known today as Ethiopia.

So it was, in that richly historic environment, that the baby boy was born, centuries after the Queen of Sheba reigned, succeeded by her son Menelik, who built a famous dynasty that lasted through the early 20th century, when Haile Selassie came to power. Selassie, who was Ethiopia's regent from 1916 to 1930, and her emperor from 1930 to 1974, claimed to be a direct descendant of King Solomon and the Queen of Sheba.

1900 was not only the beginning of a new century, but the beginning of a new gateway to international commerce. The French diplomat and entrepreneur Ferdinand de Lesseps transformed his biggest dream into reality when he and his team developed and built the Suez Canal, a massive project that changed world trading communications forever. With the canal, the route between Europe and Asia was shortened tremendously, and all the European nations were trying to establish trading posts along the Red Sea and the Indian Ocean.

Nestled in the Horn of Africa, Somaliland became a colony shared by France (French Somaliland—capital: Djibouti), England (English Somaliland—capital: Argeisha), and Italy (Italian Somaliland—capital: Mogadishu). Somaliland was a desert country without any real value, except that it was on the Road to India. It was spread along the shore of the Indian Ocean, unlike the other big countries in the area, Ethiopia and Kenya, which were inland. Ethiopia had no port, and needed one to keep up with the new commercial demands.

Fortunately, the French were building a harbor in Djibouti, where the Red Sea meets the Indian Ocean. That harbor became the last port of call for all the ships that needed to refuel and refresh supplies before entering their last stretch to Bombay and the rest of Asia—or when they returned to Europe full of Asian spices and exotic items. Djibouti became a very active harbor that made a rich country out of French Somaliland, and the Ethiopians made a deal with the French who built a railroad between Djibouti and Addis Ababa, the capital of Ethiopia. The company that built the railroad was called Le Chemin de Fer Franco-Ethiopien (CFE), and its headquarters were established in Dire Dawa, a small town located midway between Djibouti and Addis Ababa. Because of the railroad, little Dire Dawa became the most important town in Ethiopia, second only to her capital.

The colonies were a new phenomenon that presented the possibility of good fortune for many European families who could not make ends meet in their own country. They were easily seduced by these "promised lands" that offered them so much hope. At the turn of the century, many adventurous people did not hesitate to jump at the opportunity. One country that became an attractive target, even though it was not a European colony, was Ethiopia. French and Italians gradually started to settle down in this new paradise. Among them were Antonio and Gisela Stepancich who left La Bella Italia in 1912, hoping to find the quixotic pot of gold. They had two very young sons, Vasco and Carlo, and Gisela was eight months pregnant with a third child as they left Civitavecchia. They could only afford a small, slow boat; when they arrived at Port Said, the entrance of the Canal, the boat had to wait several days before it got permission to transit to Suez. While they waited, Gisela gave birth to Ada, an adorable Italian baby girl. Eventually, they completed their journey and settled down in Dire Dawa.

In Europe, the French Count Maurice de Roquefeuille, descended from a noble family, had married a woman named Adrienne, even though she was a commoner. They were very much in love, and she was very proud to have become a Countess. Madame la Comtesse, as she was called, loved music and played the piano quite well.

In those days, the movies were silent, and theaters hired pianists who could play live, and improvise music that followed the action on the screen. Adrienne was very good at it, and was hired by a few movie theaters. But the count did not think it was a good idea for a countess to play music in the darkness of a movie theater, so she stopped.

The Count lost his fortune in World War I, and found himself in a serious financial predicament. Then he remembered a mine of mica in Ethiopia that he had bought long ago. He and his wife Adrienne, in order to survive, decided to take their chances and exploit their mine. In 1926, they embarked in Marseille on their way to Ethiopia.

Their 18-year-old son Henri was left behind so he could finish his studies. But Henri was fascinated by the likes of the great French entertainers, Maurice Chevalier and Mistinguette—and he loved singing. So he started performing on the French Riviera, where they called him, "L'Enfant Chéri du Public"—"The Darling Child of the Public." He started getting some recognition. In fact, he had a hit song titled "Ragazinella" ... the piano sheet was published with his picture on the cover. It was a very funny song with play on words that, unfortunately, cannot be translated into English. Henri sang it all his life, to the delight of his friends, who asked to hear it again and again!

I still have a copy of that piano sheet, which has yellowed over the years. Sometimes, I try to sing it to my French friends, but never with the panache that my father Henri put into it. He was really talented; he was a natural.

The Military Service invited Henri to join their battalion—an offer he could not refuse! France was not at war in those days, and his Military Service did not last long. Once Henri was out of the Service, he decided to take a vacation; he set off in search of an adventure by visiting his parents in Ethiopia.

He arrived in Djibouti, took a train to Dire Dawa, and on horseback with a guide, Henri was able to track down Maurice and Adrienne's mine, located in the wilderness. The landscape was quite different from the lush Riviera. It was a new and exciting adventure for him, and he enjoyed every minute of it. The year was 1930, and he needed a job. The closest town was Dire Dawa. He went there and was hired by the CFE.

Good looking, outgoing, gifted with a good sense of humor, and playing the "Ragazinella" card everywhere he could, he became very popular with the white population, which was quite small then. He also had a way with the natives, who liked him very much. Because the CFE was a French Company, everyone in Dire Dawa was speaking French—even Ada, who studied in the only school in town run by French nuns. Her French was excellent, but with a slight Italian accent that made her roll her Rs.

One day, Henri and Ada met by chance. He was playing a tennis tournament, and she was among the spectators. The term "tennis tournament" is deceiving, however, as the few young men playing in Dire Dawa were barely able to push the ball over the net... but since no one had ever heard of 1930s French champions Lacoste and Cochet, Henri looked formidable, especially in Ada's eyes. And when Henri's eyes fell upon the gorgeous Italian girl, he went bananas, which was appropriate for the tropics! He asked her out, they got engaged... and, as in a dream, they got married. The year was 1933.

Two years later, on a showery January morning, the raindrops tap-danced loudly on the tin roof of the little clinic. In those days, the father was not allowed in the delivery room, but the clinic was so small that Henri could hear Ada crying and screaming above the storm. Suddenly, Ada's voice was silent. The doctor came out, smiled at Henri, and said, "It's a boy!"

And that's how I came to see the light of day, even though the sun was hiding behind the clouds. And that's when I found out that Ada was my mother, and Henri was my father.

CHAPTER 2

From Sheba to Lebanon

I N 1935, I suddenly found myself face to face with life... but my personal recollection of that first year is, of course, nil. I later learned that, in those days, the French, the Italians—as well as many English, Armenians, Greeks and Hindus—were helping Ethiopia modernize itself. Haile Selassie, looking to educate and develop his country, was seeking help wherever he could. Everyone got along very well... until Italian dictator Benito Mussolini decided he wanted Ethiopia for himself, and sent 250,000 troops to oust the Emperor and take over this gracious land.

War broke out. My family stayed put, being very careful not to offend anyone, but my grandfather and grandmother (the Count and Countess) returned to France. They settled down in Provence, in the charming village of Sault, on an exquisite lavender farm which would later be the joy of my adolescence.

Mussolini's army was too much for the Ethiopians—though they did, armed with spears and primitive rifles, prevail in one battle. Haile Selassie went into exile. He presented his case to the League of Nations, the precursor to the United Nations, and delivered his famous speech, in which he convinced the international community to take his side. A few years later, with the help of the League of Nations and the British Army, he returned to Addis Ababa, stronger than ever.

Peace had returned to the region, and Ethiopia was still an independent country with many foreigners in charge of developing it, particularly the French and their railroad company. My father was due a vacation, and in 1937, he took us to visit France. We embarked on a ship in Djibouti and I made my first crossing through the Suez Canal. We arrived in Marseille seven days later, at around 5 in the morning. The first thing I clearly remember about my life is looking through the porthole and seeing the lights of the big harbor. I had never seen so many lights; I was mesmerized. I don't remember anything about that first trip to France, except that, on our return to Djibouti, I crossed the Suez Canal for the second time.

Me as a little boy in Djibouti, 1938

My next memory was my fifth birthday. Our neighbors had a little girl about my age, and my mother had invited her to sit with me for an afternoon snack that included a little cake my mother had baked. I have a vivid memory of blowing out the candles and... the little girl giving me a kiss! Wow... I liked that! A good omen for things to come...

In the middle of the afternoon of June 6, 1940, my father showed up, suddenly and unexpectedly, and my mother quickly began to pack our things. Within the next few hours, we joined all the other women and children from Djibouti on a ship with people speaking a language I could not understand. My mother could not understand it, either... but she told me they were speaking English.

I learned later that, because the Germans had invaded France, an English fleet had been sent to explain the situation to the English and French colonies that did not know what was going on. In those troubled days, the technology and the communication systems were rather primitive... so, when the English asked the Governor of Djibouti to join a certain General de Gaulle heading a government in exile in London, the Governor said he had no idea who de Gaulle was, and he could not take orders from England. He wanted to hear from his own government. But that government no longer existed, and the Governor could not reach anyone. Not trusting the English, he refused to listen to them, and they threatened to blockade Djibouti. A compromise was reached, allowing the women and children to be sent to Beirut, Lebanon while Djibouti was under siege.

This was my third crossing of the Canal. At the time, by order of the League of Nations, Palestine was under British Mandate, and Lebanon was under French Mandate. That's why we were sent to Beirut, where the Free French Forces were in charge of the refugees. At first, we shared an apartment with two other women—one with two boys, and the other with a girl. It was not very comfortable.

I could feel that my mother was rather unhappy. Under normal circumstances, she was a very pretty lady, with her beautiful light brown hair, her deep brown eyes, her delicious voice that everyone enjoyed when she sang, and her very good taste in the way she dressed. But now, she had unkempt hair, no make-up, and her few outfits were wearing out very quickly. She looked like a refugee. She was very sad, and the two of us missed my father very much.

A couple of months later, the army installed us in a nice apartment with a view of the Mediterranean Sea. They gave us a little money, and our lives were more bearable. Not far from our apartment was a French school run by the Franciscan Order; I could walk to it. The fathers knew our story and were helping us make the best of it, by giving us food, books, and even a blanket.

One day, when leaving school at the end of the day, I was surprised to see some kind of white dust dancing in the air; I had never seen anything like it. I ran through the strange and beautiful atmosphere... when I arrived home, my mother told me it was snowing. It was December, but snow in Beirut was rather unusual. My first snow! I was six years old.

That's when my mother took me aside and said, "*Mon chéri*, we have no money... just enough to buy our food. I feel very bad, because I don't want to disappoint you. I wish I could have avoided this, but I have no choice. I must tell you a secret. Just between you and me. This year, Christmas will be different. You see, there is no "*Père Noël*" (the French name for Santa

Claus). The presents you found every year under the Christmas tree were not delivered by him, but by your father and me. Unfortunately, this year I cannot afford to buy you anything." She cried as she revealed the truth about a secret that was dear to children like me; she was so sorry. But that revelation did not affect me much; my mother was there, we had a nice apartment, food on the table and snow in the garden! For some reason, I was not sad. I embraced her and asked her to read me one of my favorite stories, "Petite Pluie Abat Grand Vent" ("Little Rain Calms Strong Wind"), which figuratively means that very little is needed sometimes to calm a great pain. She smiled at me and gave me a long hug. The next day in school, I felt very important, because I knew something that all the other schoolboys did not—they still believed in Santa Claus!

That's also when I met a good-looking gentleman who had become my mother's friend. He was a Christian Lebanese named Antoine Shaloub, and he was very nice to me.

At this point, even the army was unable to tell us what was happening in Djibouti, since it was blockaded by the English Fleet, and we could not get any news about my father. We did not know if he were dead or alive. The future was uncertain and rather bleak. My mother was understandably worried and confused. In time of war, nothing is secure, and her maternal instinct was to protect me. So, Antoine was for me just a friend who took my mother and me to nice restaurants, to the beach at the renowned Hotel Saint George, and to the winter slopes of the mountain called The Cedars of Lebanon, where we threw snow balls at each other.

And so, on that 1941 Christmas, when we came back home from midnight mass, I was very surprised to find a Christmas tree in the apartment, and under it, a toy that made me very happy: a little castle with a drawbridge and tin soldiers, as well as bars of chocolate (which were very difficult to find in war time). Antoine had arranged that surprise—he knew how much I liked chocolate and tin soldiers! I have never forgotten that Christmas night, and I have never forgotten Antoine, who proved how compassionate he was towards my mother and me in our time of need during that difficult period. Of course, I realized when I became an adult, that Antoine had been her temporary boyfriend who helped her make ends meet.

Years later, when I was 21, I went to Beirut on business and looked for Antoine. I found him: he was married to a lovely lady and they had a very cute little girl. His wife cooked dinner for me.

Yes, life is unpredictable, and can be beautiful, if one knows how to deal with it!

We were refugees in Beirut between 1940 and 1943. At one point, the German war planes came to bombard the harbor where French and English ships were anchored. The army sent the families in the mountains, which was a less dangerous place. We were lodged in a cute house in a little village called Bikfaya. We stayed there for quite some time. Once in a while, we would hear the far-away explosions of the bombs. My mother did not have a car, and Antoine could not leave Beirut. But he found a way to visit us a couple of times, to make sure that we did not need anything. My mother and I walked a lot, happy to pick berries and pine cones along the paths, breathing freely the soft scent of rosemary and thyme. My mother and I became very close during this challenging time.

One day, we were awakened by a loud noise coming from

the dirt road in front of our house. We went out and, to our surprise, a long caravan of soldiers on motorcycles and jeeps rolled past us, right in front of our eyes. The soldiers were wearing big hats with one side pulled up. My mother said that they were Australian soldiers. We waved at them, we screamed hello and welcome to them, we were jumping with joy, knowing that they came to protect us. They waved back at us, laughing and responding with great warmth. They were our first Australians, and they made us feel so secure! Suddenly, they were gone... but that night, my mother and I slept very well.

When things calmed down, we returned to our apartment in Beirut. One day, Antoine took us to the little beach at the Saint George Hotel and I went into the water, trying to swim while making sure my feet could still touch the bottom. There was a jetty along the beach; the water was deep on the far side of jetty, and only good swimmers could dive there. Antoine was watching me have fun on the shallow side of the jetty. He called to me, and I went with him. He took me in his arms... and threw me in the water on the deep side of the jetty! I screamed, I struggled—and suddenly realized that I could swim! Antoine had seen me stay on top of the water on the safe side without touching the bottom, so he knew that I would not drown. That's how I learned how to swim at the Saint George Hotel in Beirut—at least, it's where I learned how to stay on top of the water without drowning!

I often went to the movies while we lived in Beirut; I saw all Hollywood films. I was captivated by the likes of Tyrone Power and Henry Fonda in "Jesse James," Tyrone Power and Linda Darnell in "The Mark of Zorro," Clark Gable and Vivian Leigh in "Gone with the Wind," and of course, "Snow White." The action captured on the screen, the beauty of the actresses, the environment that was so different than anything I knew... so many things about those films fascinated me. An idea was born in the back of my mind that would develop along the years. It was not yet exactly clear... but I knew then that I wanted to go to Hollywood!

The Beirut episode suddenly came to an end when we learned that Djibouti had surrendered, and that we had to go back. All the women and children had to go to Suez to board a ship. For my mother, and another woman who had two boys my age, the army put at our disposal a big American car and a little truck for the luggage. It was 1943, and we were off...

CHAPTER 3

Cairo

W E LEFT Beirut very early in the morning to avoid the heat of the desert sun, traveling through Palestine and crossing the Sinai Desert. Our destination was Cairo, Egypt, where we would wait for a ship to be ready for us in Suez. The desert can be quite inhospitable in the last week of May. I was eight years old, and I could feel that something unusual was happening. I understood that at the end of this journey, we were going to see my father who was very much alive, and my heart was beating with joy. But there was a certain apprehension in the air, and I was uneasy. I could not close my eyes; the window of the car was open because there was no air conditioning, and I kept looking out as we traversed the vast, barren desert.

The road from Lebanon to Palestine was mainly a dirt road, and we were driving at a snail's pace. After a couple of hours, the sun slowly started rising. It was around 7 in the morning, and the Lebanese driver decided to stop for breakfast at a little café on top of a hill. I remember that very well... and that, when we got out of the car, the Mediterranean Sea was sparkling in front of us. Along its shore was what looked like a large city. We asked the owner of the café what town that was. He said: "That? It's Tel-Aviv!"

I was really enjoying our adventure. I had a big bowl of

café au lait with *tartines* and butter, which was rare during the war. I do not remember exactly how long we stayed at the café on the hill, and where we went after that enchanting breakfast, but I remember clearly that, later on, I was again in the car, in the middle of the Sinai Desert, the night surrounding us. My head was again out the window, gazing at the infinite, hypnotic landscape, this lifeless piece of earth, and I tried to understand why there were no houses, no trees, not a soul anywhere to be seen. Only two vehicles were rolling in the massive desert under a myriad of stars, traveling through the expanse of the universe. But, even though it felt a little scary, a full moon made everything luminous. In the silence of the night, my mother whispered, "It looks like we are on the moon!"

That's when the other lady traveling with us noticed a rifle next to the driver. She asked him why he was carrying a gun in the car. He said there had been some incidents in the past year in which "bandits" attacked people in the desert, and he had been advised to bring a gun to protect us. My mother asked him who the bandits were. He said, "I am told that they are some Jewish people." We now know that when Palestine was under British Mandate, paramilitary actions were carried out by Jewish underground groups against the British, who did not keep their promise, under the 1917 Balfour Declaration, to secure a Jewish National Home in Palestine. We were driving through the desert in the middle of the night, never imagining that five years later, it would become the State of Israel! Fortunately, nothing happened... and the next day, around noon, we finally arrived in Cairo.

We were very tired, but a French gentleman—I believe he was an official from the French Consulate—greeted us at a fancy hotel. He tried to make all of us feel welcome... and, as our liaison, he gave us some good news about Djibouti. Everyone was fine and waiting for us. But we still had to wait until a ship was ready to depart from Suez.

We went to our room on the third floor, and were pleasantly surprised: it was a beautiful room with a big bed, and the décor was very elegant. It was my first hotel room, and I thought that I was in Paradise! We lay down and immediately fell asleep. Around 7 p.m., the phone rang and my mother answered. The French gentleman who'd greeted us was inviting all the ladies to dinner, compliments of the French Army.

In 1943, Cairo was already quite a bustling city. It was not affected by the war, and was full of refugees from all over Europe. I remember that the hotel, the streets, and the restaurants were very crowded. But on that first night, while our mothers were off to dinner, the kids had to stay in their rooms where we were fed and put to bed. Of course, I could not sleep. Then, I heard a big sound coming from the street, loud voices speaking that language I could not understand. I got up and looked out the window. Across from the hotel was an open-air movie theater, and from my window, I could see the movie projected on the big screen. I left my room and knocked on the door of the two other boys' room. They followed me to my room, and the three of us, leaning our arms on the windowsill, watched with delight as Gary Cooper and Paulette Goddard performed for us in "Northwest Mounted Police."

We stayed in Cairo for about three or four days, then drove about 140 km to Suez to board our ship; since we were riding alongside the canal in a car, I considered that it was my fourth canal crossing. We were again on an English ship, but some officers could speak French, and we were so impressed to speak with these men in uniforms! Another memory from that trip: grapefruits. I had never before eaten a grapefruit, and every morning in our cabin, the steward brought two half grapefruits. In those days, grapefruits were very bitter, so we sprinkled a lot of sugar on them, and I loved it!

Our ship entered the harbor of Djibouti on June 6, 1943, three years to the day since we had left. After we docked, everyone leaned over the rails, trying to find our fathers and husbands on the pier. Suddenly, I heard a voice yell my nickname: "Popaul! Popaul!!!" I looked down, and there was my father, smiling under his pith helmet, looking handsome in his khaki shorts and white shirt—the uniform in the colonies. Even though I had not seen my father in three years, I recognized him right away, and screamed, "Papa! Papa!" My mother squeezed my shoulders. Tears glistened on her cheeks.

CHAPTER 4

Djibouti

I WOULD spend my next three years in Djibouti, during which I attended a nun school, passed my "Certificat d'Etudes Primaires" and saw more movies made in Hollywood. I found myself dreaming of climbing skyscrapers, of dancing with Fred Astaire and Ginger Rodgers, of discovering The Treasure of the Sierra Madre, and of singing with Shirley Temple, Judy Garland and my favorite guy, Mickey Rooney—I really wanted to be like him (maybe a little taller)! And my father was always telling me that I'd better have good grades if I wanted to go see a Mickey Rooney movie—some incentive!

One day in school, the nun who was our teacher decided to ask us what we wanted to do later in life. When she asked me, I said, "I want to be a movie star." The nun almost fainted! The Mother Superior was not too happy, either, and even contacted my parents to complain. I don't know what words were exchanged in their meeting, but I had to promise that I would never again say that... to a nun!

I had to start somewhere, and if Hollywood was beyond my reach, I found that singing was more accessible to me. My father had several 78 rpm records of Charles Trenet, who was then the greatest singer-composer in France. He wrote classic songs that also became popular in America, such as "Beyond The Sea" and "I Wish You Love." We had a phonograph that we cranked manually with a handle. Since we did not have a radio, the only music I could listen to came from these records. I listened over and over to several Trenet songs—"Le Soleil et La Lune" ("The Sun and the Moon"), "Je Chante" ("I Sing"), "Y'A D'La Joie" ("There Is Joy"), "Boum!" ("Boom!"), "Mam'zelle Clio," ("Miss Clio"), "Le Grand Café" ("The Big Café"), and so many others. They were all masterpieces. For some reason, I had learned by heart "Le Grand Café," and I was having fun singing it in front of the mirror of my parents's bedroom armoire.

My father Henri had enjoyed a short career as a singer on the French Riviera, and he always kept his talent alive in front of friends and on special occasions, such as charity balls. During the blockade, the governor had asked him to put together some shows to keep up the morale of the population. These shows were extremely successful, and earned my father a special decoration from the government. He became kind of famous in Djibouti, and the governor asked him every year to organize the Red Cross Ball. He would put together some shows in which he and my mother would sing, joined by a couple of other people who used to sing for him in the blockade shows.

One night, my father came home and caught me singing in front of the mirror. After listening to me he said, "I'll put you in the Red Cross Show this year." I was so excited! On the day of the ball, my mother dressed me in a suit and tie. That night, there I was, watching the people in tuxedos and evening dresses dancing to the music of 78 rpm records. At one point, my father went to the microphone and announced the beginning of the show. He said, "We have a new face in the show this year—he is a young singer with a promising talent. He is going to sing for you a Charles Trenet song, 'Le Grand Café.' Here he is: Popaul!"

I was eight years old, and as cool as anyone can be in a tropical setting. I had no fear. I got on the stage, I sang a cappella, all by myself, and when the song ended, all the pretty women came around me to congratulate me and give me lots of kisses! Wow! All I had to do was sing a song, and the women were kissing me? I knew right there that I was going to be a singer!

I was doing other fun things those days. On certain Sunday mornings, my parents and a group of their friends used to rent a boat and head for a small island called Maskali. In those days, the Red Sea was crystal clear; I was fascinated by the many fish of all colors swimming around the pink coral lying at the bottom. Dolphins would dance gracefully around the boat... I swear, they were smiling at me!

On the way to Maskali, we would fish. My father taught me how to cast the line and wait for the fish to bite. It was a good lesson in patience and psychology: do not rush, take your time, let the fish take the bait, let him believe that the shrimp at the end of the hook is his dessert, and when he bites... reel him in! The fish used to bite so fast that in less than one hour, we would catch more than enough for everyone's lunch. On the island, where the sand was so fine and so white that it looked like flour, the men built the fire and the women cooked the *bouillabaisse*.

While the cooking was in progress, we would all go to the side of the beach where the sea had created an overhang by eroding the bottom of the wall of rocks, forming a tidal cave where we could stand with the water at our waist, protected from the sun. The ceiling of the cave was encrusted with oysters. We would reach up, crack the shell with a stone, and standing on tip toes, suck out the delicious morsels. Someone always brought some cold white wine that everybody shared... even me!

My Italian grandparents, Gisela and Antonio, were still in Dire Dawa, and each summer we visited them for a couple of months. They were adorable; I always looked forward to that trip. Also, the summers in Djibouti were so hot that it was a relief to get away from that terrible heat and breathe the slightly cooler Ethiopian air. We would spend a couple of weeks in Dire Dawa, then go to Harar, an old town high in the mountains where the air was really pure. Harar dated from the Middle Ages. It was surrounded by ramparts which were starting to crumble. Its main street was about 7 feet wide. It used to be a mercantile center, and merchants with their camels caravans used to come there from everywhere. There was a very nice hotel that had been built by the Italians, and we would stay there for at least a month.

One thing that made our stay there more exciting for me was the fact that the visionary French poet Arthur Rimbaud had spent the end of his life there. Rimbaud wrote two revolutionary books of poems and prose when he was in his late teens. His most famous poems are *Le Bateau Ivre* (*The Drunken Boat*) and *Une Saison en Enfer* (*A Season in Hell*). He was the toast of Paris, and became the lover of celebrated French symbolist poet Paul Verlaine, who was married and much older. They led a wild life that scandalized the Parisian literary coterie. But their torrid love affair turned into a nightmare. Rimbaud, tired of the bourgeoisie of Paris, and fed up with getting high on absinthe and hashish, gave up writing and decided to travel around the world. He ended up in Harar and lived with an Ethiopian mistress who taught him the ecstasy of love with a woman.

My other grandfather, the Count, told me in later years that he had been invited in the 1920's to a formal dinner given in

Harar to honor the Emperor Haile Selassie. The event took place at the Palace of one of the Emperor's sons, Prince Makonnen. During the evening, he met Monseigneur Jarousseau, who had been the archbishop for the Ethiopian territory since 1888. The archbishop told my grandfather that he had known Rimbaud, but never suspected that he was such a famous writer with such a stormy past. In fact, Rimbaud had become a little merchant on his own, and lived a quiet life. Even though he developed a friendship with Ras Makonnen, who was the father of future Emperor Haile Selassie, Rimbaud's social life was rather non-existent, and he obviously missed the cultural atmosphere of Paris. Eventually he became very sick, returned to France, and died in Marseille in 1891, at age 37. He is today considered one of the most fascinating and imaginative French writers, and the most chimerical writer of French literature.

A caravan was supposed to bring all of Rimbaud's belongings from Harar to Djibouti to be put on a ship for Marseille, but that caravan was looted and never reached its destination. Therefore, we will never know if Rimbaud wrote anything while in Ethiopia. Years later, when I studied his work in school, I dreamed that someday an archeologist would find pieces of paper under a rock, in the wilderness between Harar and Djibouti, in the same way that the Dead Sea scrolls were discovered, and realize that it was the last writings of that untamed poet... so far, no archeologist has made my dream come true!

A couple of times, we visited what we were told was Rimbaud's house in Harar; unfortunately, it was in a dire state, without any evidence of his presence. It was just an old house very badly cared for by the current residents.

Prince Makonnen, Haile Selassie's second son, spent his

summer vacations in Harar, where he had a discreet palace with big cages that held a couple of lions. The cages were hidden behind the wall surrounding the palace. We could not see the beasts, but it was thrilling to be awakened sometimes in the middle of the night by the loud roar of these sovereigns of the animal kingdom.

The prince had learned about my father's organization of the Red Cross Balls in Djibouti, and asked him if he would be willing to do the same thing in Harar. Of course, Henri agreed, and I remember one summer when he put together a show for that event. I did not sing, but the prince had put at our disposal a luxurious chauffeured American limousine, chocolate brown around the sides and beige on top. My first limousine... it was really awesome! And when we were inside the limo, riding to the ball, I looked at my parents with admiration, and they smiled at me.

In the early morning of June 6, 1944, I went to my school in Djibouti, just like every other day. We were in class less than five minutes when the Mother Superior materialized in front of us, as if from nowhere. We only saw her once a week on Saturday afternoons when she came to give us our grades, so her appearance that morning really surprised us, it was so unusual. We wondered what could make her come so early on this Tuesday morning. She sat down at the desk, smiled at us—which was also very unusual—and said, "My children, I was trying to listen to the radio this morning but it was very difficult to hear in the midst of the crackling sounds of the airwaves. However, I believe that I heard that something very important is happening in France. It seems that the Allied Forces have started an invasion to liberate France from the German domination. I think I heard that the invasion is taking place on the Mediterranean Coast. Whatever it is, something big is happening, and I give you the day off to spend with your parents on this historic occasion."

The communications were very primitive in those days, nd very few people owned a radio. The kids in my class and I were all about 9 years old, and not very aware of what was happening in Europe; we knew there was a war, but not much more. So, we did not really comprehend what the Mother Superior was telling us... but we *did* understand that we had the day off!

I ran home. When I arrived, my mother greeted me with an incredulous look in her eyes, thinking that I had sneaked out of school.

"What are you doing here? You should be in school!"

I could feel that she was a little upset, so I whispered with hesitation, "I don't know... uh... the... Mother Superior said... uh... we had the day off..."

"What are you talking about? The day off? Why?"

"I don't know."

As I started to cry, my father arrived home.

"You, too?" My mother said, "What's going on?"

And my father explained it to her. She took me in her arms and kissed me. It was a very moving moment.

We spent the rest of the day at the home of my father's boss. He had a radio, and we gathered around it, trying to understand what the situation was. The sound faded in and out, so we really had to pay close attention. As the sun was caressing the horizon, it had finally become clear that the American Forces had landed in Normandy, and that the Germans were retreating. We were all dancing with joy, emotionally overtaken by a sense of relief. The boss opened his fridge, and suddenly, the champagne was flowing. My father gave me a cup and said: "Drink, my boy; you will never forget this day." He was right: I never forgot that on D-Day, I drank my first cup of champagne!

Two months after that celebration, my mother and I went to Dire Dawa, and then to Harar, as we did every summer. There were other mothers and children there, and we all knew each other very well. Every year, our fathers would join us to spend a week in Harar to breathe a little fresh air; they deserved a respite from working hard in the torrid heat of Djibouti.

Some of the other children and I decided to put a show together to surprise our parents; we rehearsed every day until our fathers arrived.

On August 25, we invited all our parents to see our show. At about 4 in the afternoon, they all came, sat down, and we started the show. Suddenly, right in the middle of one of my songs, the hotel manager came to my father and they both left the room. I was humiliated and very disturbed that my father walked out during the show that had required so much effort by all the children. I could see that my mother was also quite concerned.

A few minutes later, my father came back, jumped on the stage and stopped the show. Now, I was really upset. But then, my father spoke to the audience: "My dear friends, I have the most wonderful news. We just learned that the Allied Forces have entered Paris! Paris has been liberated! The Germans have surrendered! Paris is free!!!"

Everyone jumped to their feet, and burst into applause and screams of joy... it was a total pandemonium, and everyone left the room to celebrate, leaving all the children standing on the stage, with our mouths opened, looking at each other in disbelief. How dare they interrupt our show just because Paris was free! It wasn't until later that we finally understood the magnitude and the historical significance of that event.

In September, it was time to go back to school. I had to study hard, because the following year I had to pass my exam called *Le Certificat d'Etudes Primaires*, which I did successfully. Since there was no school above that primary school in Djibouti, and since my parents wanted to give me a good education, they decided to send me to France.

Now that the war was over, communications had improved, and my father wrote to my grandparents, the Count and Countess, to find a college where I could pursue my studies. It so happened that there was a famous Jesuit boarding school near their home in Sault, The College Saint Joseph, located in the town of Avignon, celebrated for its *Palais des Papes* (The Popes' Palace). The palace was built in 1335, when the catholic religion split and there were two popes—one in Rome and one in Avignon—and is one of the largest and most important medieval Gothic buildings in Europe.

My parents made the necessary arrangements, and in August 1946, I left Djibouti for Avignon. I was 11 years old.

CHAPTER 5

Sault

M Y PARENTS were not rich. They were making a big sacri-
fice to finance my studies at the expensive College Saint
Joseph, so they certainly could not afford to send me first class!
So, they booked me on a freighter, and I had to sleep on the deck
in a hammock. I carried only one valise, which was locked and
rested under my hammock. I was not worried about it, since
it contained nothing of real value—just my toiletries and my
underwear. Whatever I needed for the boarding school would
be found in France.

My parents had taught me how to be careful, how to take
care of my belongings, how to behave with strangers, and how
to stay out of trouble. And my father entrusted me with a special
item: a gold coin (I believe it was a Krugerrand) to give the
Count and my grandmother, to help them take care of me. That
was a valuable item, and we had to make sure nobody could
steal it from me. My mother came up with the solution: she
asked me to wear my best socks, and to slip the coin between
the sock and the bottom of my foot—which meant I had to keep
the same socks night and day until I reached Marseille.

On the day of my departure, my parents took me to the
freighter, chose my hammock with the officer in charge, and
asked him to look after me. Then, the moment came when we

had to say *au revoir*. I tried to listen to their last instructions, but my eyes were full of tears. My mother also was crying. It was the first time that my mother and I would be separated, and my heart was quite heavy. But deep inside, we knew that going to France was the right thing for me. So we took our courage in our hands, and with my dad's help, we regained our composure. After a long embrace, they left the ship, and the ship left Djibouti.

The trip took around seven days. Every time I got in or out of the hammock, I was very careful that my socks were in place, and I tried not to limp when I walked. Needless to say, a long bath would be welcome when I arrived in France!

I crossed the Suez Canal for the fifth time. And one early morning, I saw the lights of Marseille—this time, from the deck. I had to go through the customs formalities, and of course, they did not dare to ask this kid to take his socks off... if only to avoid the smell!

My grandmother Adrienne was there at the dock, waiting for me. She had not seen me since I was 2, and kept looking at me. After a few hugs, it was time to go to Sault. She was 60 years old, and the war had not been kind to her. She and Maurice could barely make ends meet; she wore no makeup, her face was deeply wrinkled, the gray in her hair made her look dirty, she was wearing a long black woolen skirt and a heavy black sweater that were too big for her. On top of all that, she wore one of those shawls that an inelegant grandma would wear in the movies. If Central Casting had needed an old Italian peasant woman, she would have been on top of the list. She certainly did not look like a countess. But she was my father's mother, my grandmother, and I smiled at her with respect, even though in the following years, I never could connect emotionally with her.

We took several bus rides through Aix-en-Provence, Avignon, Salon, and Carpentras... finally, we arrived in that picturesque lavender farm where Maurice, the Count, had prepared a delicious roasted chicken with sautéed champignons cèpes, which grew in the woods behind the farm. He was a very distinguished gentleman in his late sixties, very cultured, very logical, very sensible; he taught me how to think. But he had one flaw: to the consternation of my grandmother, he did not know how to make money. He had been raised without having to earn money, other than what came regularly to him from his family properties before WW I. Noblesse oblige! So now, he could just survive with what the farm was producing. Through the years, between the boarding school and Sault, where I spent my vacations, we talked about everything: from politics, to art, to women... but the subject of money never came up. He was a very important influence in my life, and I became very fond of him.

Once, and only once, he told me a story that happened in 1942. Because of the strategic location of the little village of Sault, which was very difficult to access, the region became a nest for the Maquis— the name of the French Resistance during WWII. Sault became the center of *La Résistance* for that region. That's why many Jewish refugees who tried to avoid or to escape the concentration camps were guided through Sault after leaving Switzerland. The Maquis had organized a very good network to help them reach Spain and Portugal, where they could board a ship for the United States. But the escape route was risky, and they had to hide them in secure places owned by people they could trust. Maurice was very proud to have been chosen as a stopover. The farm became a hiding place, and Maurice and his wife fed those refugees on many occasions. But it was a secret, as it was dangerous to trust anyone, even in Sault... even after the war! In September of 1946, Maurice drove me to the College Saint Joseph in Avignon.

CHAPTER 6

Avignon

I WAS NOW a boarder in a respected school in Avignon. As
you may know, the Jesuits are excellent educators, but they
are very strict disciplinarians. At first it was difficult for me,
because I was a free spirit who had traveled a lot for my age, I
was very independent, and I did not like being forced to walk
along the walls of the corridors, in rank and in silence. I was
kind of a rebel and my disciplinary grades were not the best!
But all the students liked me. They had never met anybody
born in Africa, and they nicknamed me *L'Africain*: The African.
"Popaul" disappeared, and "The African" was born!

I had good grades in school—not in math, but in History,
Geography, Latin, Greek, English and French Composition. In
fact, the subject of the first composition I had to write was: "What
were you doing when the Americans landed in Normandy?" I
told the story of the Mother Superior, and earned first place! My
teacher thought it was very original, very creative. But all I did
was to relate the events as they happened—and I did not have
to be a rocket scientist to do that. But it allowed me to always
be classified number one or two or three of the best students in
my class.

And then, there was soccer. I had an affinity for the position
of goal keeper, and I became quite good at it, and was selected

to be the goal keeper of the Junior South-East team of France. The country was divided into four divisions (what would be called in the States, High School Divisions), and for my age group category, there was a championship each year. The year I was selected, I was a very proud and confident 15 years old. But the day we played for the championship, the Mistral wind that comes from the Alps and gains speed coming down the Rhône Valley, was blowing strongly. *Le Mistral* is well known in Provence; everyone will tell you it can be dangerous. In the first half of the game, the wind kept the players on the other side of the field; all I had to do was try to keep warm. The wind made it almost impossible to control the ball, and my team did not score. Then, in the second half, I got very busy! I had twenty players within ten to twenty feet in front of me, and it was not easy to see the ball. We played defense aggressively, until a gust of wind curved the ball in my net, and there was nothing I could do... so, we lost by one goal. Damn that Mistral!

The year of my 15th birthday, my parents came to France on a holiday. It was springtime, and I had one week of vacation for Easter. I took the train to meet them in Marseille. On the first night, we went to the theater to see a musical comedy. I do not remember what musical comedy it was, but I remember that I fell in love with the pretty female singer who seemed to sing just for me! And when the fat tenor kissed her, my imagination took over, and I knew that one day, I would be the one she would like to kiss!

The next day, we had lunch in a special restaurant that only served seafood. We ordered "un plateau de fruits de mer." Translated literally, it means a tray of fruits from the sea, but it is simply a tray of sea food (the French have always had a tendency to give poetic names to their food!). Delicious oysters of all sizes and tastes were included, and we enjoyed them; they reminded us of the little ones we used to suck up on the rocks of Maskali.

One evening, my father took me aside to talk to me about the birds and the bees. He said something that stayed with me all my life: "My son, you are a man, now. You will have several encounters with women. They are very different from us, and sometimes you may not understand them. But I am asking you to always remember that women give birth to the world. They are lovely and very special. Without them, life would be boring and pointless. Take good care of them and love them with great tenderness, always... even if they talk too much!" Yes, Dad, I have followed your advice, and it made my life very exciting!

One very important thing happened in my last year at the College Saint Joseph, in my Philosophy class. The Jesuit priest, le Père Franchet, who was liked and respected by all the students, started the class by saying, "Today, we are going to study the idea of God. Who is God? During the war, on the battle front, at dawn before the attack, a French priest was blessing the troops and encouraging them with words like, 'My children, be courageous, go and fight for France, I bless you, do not be afraid, go and fight, God is with you!' Now, on the German side, a German priest was also telling his troops, 'Do not be afraid, I bless you, God is with you!' So, who was God with?"

At that moment, a light flashed in my brain and changed my life forever. In a second, I understood that God is no more with the Germans than He is with the French, no more with the Chinese than He is with the Congolese, no more with the Christians than He is with the Jews, no more with the Muslims than He is with the Buddhists. I understood that we are all His children and that He is not with anyone in particular and that He certainly is not with any religion in particular. It became very clear to me that, if everyone understood that simple truth, we would have no more wars, since religion has always been one of the reasons that started all the wars, since the beginning of time. Millions of people have died so needlessly in the name of religion. Then, I suddenly remembered something that happened in Djibouti when I was 9 years old: a friend of my parents who was an amateur magician had taught me some magic tricks, and I was quite good at it. In fact, I even impressed my father with a trick that consisted of swallowing a knife!

Every Friday, an Arab fisherman came to our house to sell his fish. His name was Ahmed; he was a very nice man, but completely uneducated. His simple life consisted of taking his small boat to sea before dawn, catching his fish, selling it from house to house, and at the end of the day, eating and going to bed early. He did not know anything else. One Friday, when Ahmed arrived at our house, my father said: "Look, Ahmed: Popaul is going to swallow a knife!" When I performed the trick, Ahmed froze. He had never seen a trick before, and he believed that I had really swallowed the knife. To my amazement, he threw himself to the ground and bowed down in front of me, in the manner the Muslims bow down to Allah; he believed that I was God. And every Friday after that, when he came to our house, he would bow down in front of me and never again dared to look at me in the eyes. It was the most extraordinary behavior I had ever witnessed.

Thinking of that experience in association with what le Père Franchet had said, I realized that we have no idea of whom or what God is. It is that unknown factor behind the Universe, behind the sun and the hurricanes, behind the joys and the stars, behind the toys and the wars, behind the galaxies and the black holes, behind the love and the hate, behind the lovers and the flowers, behind the arrow and the rainbow. It is The Mystery that we will never solve. Those who pretend to know Him or talk to Him are just charlatans who only take advantage of the weak for personal profits. Yes, there is One God, the God of the Universe, not the God of religions. For me, it is Mother Nature. Le Père Franchet is dead now, but I will never stop thanking him for opening my mind, and I think of him every night when I pray with that simple prayer: "Who ever You are, What ever You are, Wherever You are, YOU ARE and I believe in you. I thank You for the life you are giving me." And I do not need a church or a temple or a mosque to say that.

During my seven years at the College Saint Joseph, I had the pleasure of making some friends who are still my friends today. First, since my parents were in Djibouti and my grandparents were in Sault, no one could visit me on Sundays. There were other guys in the same quandary; for us, the Jesuits came up with a plan in which people living in Avignon could, by special arrangement with the parents, become our "correspondents." I became very friendly with one of the students by the name of Jean-Pierre Barret. He talked to his parents, who wrote to my parents, and that's how the Barrets became my correspondents. They had a lovely apartment close to the college. On Sundays, if my discipline grades permitted it, they would receive me with great warmth, they would feed me, and they would sometimes take me to the movies. Jean-Pierre's father was crazy about the American movies, and was a big fan of Humphrey Bogart. So, with their help, I continued my love affair with the Hollywood mystique. Of course, Jean-Pierre also loved the American films; when I would see him during my annual vacation in France, our main subject of discussion would be the latest movies with George Clooney, Julia Roberts, Jack Nicholson, Angelina Jolie, Leonardo DiCaprio, Clint Eastwood, and Jane Fonda. Jean-Pierre knew the release dates of all the classic films, with the names of all the stars of days gone by. My good friend had three wonderful grown children, and was a happy man. Unfortunately, his wife of 50 years died in 2014, and the next year, he had a surgery during which a mistake was made, and his entire left side became paralyzed. His daughters live in Tahiti, and brought him to their home, and he went through a lot of special exercises that did not help him much. But he kept up his morale, and when we would speak on the phone, he joked that he was listening to Bing Crosby and Bob Hope singing to Dorothy Lamour under the palm trees of Tahiti!

Recently, a dreadful news came from his daughters; Jean-Pierre passed away peacefully. He was my first close friend of many, many years to leave this world. He was 82, and it was a very painful moment for me. Now that he is back with his wife, his mother and his father, we hope that he is happy. But I will miss him.

Jean-Louis Vidal-Revel, another close friend whose parents lived on the Riviera in Nice, also became very important in my life. On a few occasions, his parents had invited me to spend some time in Nice at Christmas, or during *Le Carnaval de Nice*, a big event in France. His elder sister Claude was always making sure that I was well taken care of. I had such a good time with them. Many years later, when my parents retired in Nice, Jean-Louis, who owned a couple of apartment buildings, asked my father if he was interested in supervising their maintenance, and in smoothing the relations with the tenants. Henri was getting bored doing nothing, and accepted with enthusiasm. My parents moved to a beautiful apartment in one of Jean-Louis' buildings, and stayed there until they passed away.

Since I was in Los Angeles, it was not always easy for me to go to Nice, but Jean-Louis was always there to take care of my parents when they needed something, and I will always be deeply grateful to him for being such a loyal friend. There are not too many like him! He is married, has a son who is a famous news anchor on TV, and of course, we still see each other when I go to Nice.

One last story about my time in boarding school. It happened the last night I was there, after I had successfully passed the year-end exam which was then called the *baccalauréat*. I had been singing in several events such as fund raisers for the college, and I was a kind of "star" in the student body. And since the Jesuits were very strict, all the doors were locked at night. But in that last year, a couple of my pals and I had become more daring; we had found a way to sneak out once in a while, to grab a glass of wine in a café and smell the perfumed scent of the women around us. One Sunday, I learned that Radio Monte-Carlo, which was a popular radio station, was going to be in Avignon for the elimination of a singing competition that was held all around France. I entered the contest. There was one problem: it was taking place on the last night that I had to spend in the boarding school. But since it was my last night, I did not mind taking a risk, and sneaked out to participate. I sang one song—and I won! I got back to school just in time to go to bed with the other students. The next morning, we all had to attend our farewell mass. Coming out of the chapel, we were hugging the walls of the corridor in rank and in silence for the last time. The father who was in charge of disciplining us was in the middle of the corridor with a rolled newspaper in his hands. As I was passing by him, he called me and said, "Please join me in my office." That did not sound good!

He sat in his chair, opened the paper, handed it to me, and said, "Can you explain that?" One of the headlines in the paper read: A STUDENT FROM THE COLLEGE SAINT JOSEPH WINS THE RADIO MONTE-CARLO CONTEST. Of course, the article mentioned my name. I was petrified. I mumbled that I was sorry, and he said in a severe tone, "We trusted you, we liked you, but you sneaked out without permission, you broke the rules, you were disobedient, and you are very lucky that it is the last day. I could have expelled you. You can go now."

As I was walking through the door of his office for the last time, he called me back. I turned around. To my surprise, he was smiling. He said, "I would also like to offer you my congratulations for winning that contest. We are proud of you." And with these last words from the commander in chief, I left the College Saint Joseph d'Avignon!

A couple of weeks later, the final contest for the Southern region of France was held in Marseille. For the first time, I was singing in front of a large audience, in a big theatre. For the first time, I found out what being nervous meant. My mouth was very dry, and my legs were shaking. I don't remember how I sang—but I remember that I did not win.

CHAPTER 7

Danielle

SINCE I have decided to reveal most of my intimate secrets, I must interject here the glorious story of how I lost my virginity!

In the summer of 1951, I was 16 years old. School ended the last week in June, and I went to Sault, as I did for most of my summer vacations. On Sunday mornings, my grandmother and I went to church for Sunday mass, and I would wear what we called then my "Sunday suit." Many people thought that I was kind of cute and quite mature for my age. After mass, we would go to the Hotel du Louvre, which had a lovely terrace on the quaint plaza in front of the church, to drink a glass of lemonade.

One Sunday, I learned that the hotel had opened a little room in the back, where every Saturday evening, people could dance to the sound of American records, which were very difficult to find after the war. The next Saturday, I went there to check out what was happening, and to listen to some music. These evenings were attended by people in their 20's and 30's, and two or three kids like me. We were all enthralled by the sounds of Glenn Miller, Tommy Dorsey, Frank Sinatra, Nat King Cole, Count Basie and the Andrew Sisters, among others, as they were very new to us. They brought romantic fantasy to our young ears.

That Saturday, the summer evening was absolutely beautiful. The smell of jasmine was floating in the air, and the temperature was delicious. Among the customers was a young lady named Danielle, who spent a couple of weeks vacation in Sault every summer, to get away from her stressful activities in Paris, and her married life. She knew me as a kid; I had met her many times in the previous years. She was so pretty, that she had very often danced in my dreams. That particular evening, she was sitting across the room from me, alone. The lights were very low, and I did not think she could see me. I kept looking at her as if she was Brigitte Bardot.

The dance floor was crowded with dancers who were quite flirtatious with each other. Sinatra was singing, "Night and day, you are the one…" Danielle got up, walked across the floor to me, and said, "Oh, Jean-Paul, you are no longer a little boy; you look great. Would you dance with me?"

I was frozen in time! She took my hand and pulled me to the dance floor. I followed her and took her in my arms, holding her at a distance. But without a word, she pulled me against her, cheek to cheek, and kept squeezing my hand. This could not be real… my mind was flying. I was suddenly a Chagall lover! I finally was able to stutter, "I don't… uh… I don't know… uh… what to say." She whispered, "You don't have to say a thing. All you have to do is get on your bicycle tomorrow morning around noon and we'll go for a ride. I'll bring lunch." "Lunch?" I was puzzled. "Yes," she said, "we may have to eat something."

The next morning was Sunday, and I had to go to mass. The priest's sermon seemed to have no end; I could not wait to get out of the church. After mass, I told my grandmother that I was going for a ride on my own, and that I would meet her later at the farm. I jumped on my bicycle, and rode to the place Danielle and I had agreed upon.

It was July. The sky was wearing a light blue shirt for the occasion. The warm air was full of passion. The red poppies and the yellow buttercups were the colors in a Renoir painting. The lavender fields surrounding Sault were proud to show us their magnificent complexion, and to intoxicate us with their unique scent that wafted around us.

Danielle and I went riding. We were a few miles away from Sault when she stopped and guided me to the only tree standing in the middle of a field of wheat—a large oak who had seen many centuries go by, and possibly many lovers. I looked at her. She was wearing a simple linen shirt that was opened to the third or fourth button. It was obvious there were no bra under it. Her short skirt in light, flowing cotton caressed her hips. Suddenly, her beautiful smile hit me in the face. Under her long black hair, her green eyes talked to me, hypnotized me. She said, "Don't you want to kiss me?" Those magic words awakened me. I took her in my arms and tasted her sensual red lips; a taste that has stayed with me all my life. It was the taste of desire, that unique taste that I had been dreaming about, and that I was discovering for the first time. It was a long kiss!

She left my arms and spread a blanket under the tree. We sat down, very close to each other. My heart was dancing the jitterbug, and my brain stopped functioning. Now, another part of my being was thinking for me. She was so feminine. With the voice of an angel, she offered me a sandwich... but I was not hungry for a sandwich! My 16-year-old body was like a volcano ready to explode. She was a 24-year-old beauty on a mission. She understood. We left the sandwiches to the ants, and as if she were conducting a symphony, she opened for me the dazzling gates to paradise. The opening of these gates beat mass any day! She made me discover the scent of a woman, the taste of a woman. She taught me well. Our bodies were moving to the music of our senses. The song "C'est Si Bon" came to my mind. And in that instant, we became one. In that moment, we were alone in the universe.

And that's how the kid became the man who followed me through life.

When I got back to the farm my grandmother asked, "Where have you been? What were you doing?" I said, "I was riding... oh, yes, I was riding... and I reached the Heavens." She thought I was crazy, but the Count looked at me with understanding in his eyes and a discreet smile on his face.

I tried to see Danielle again, but the next day was July 14, Bastille Day, and her husband had come to surprise her. In the evening, there was an orchestra on the plaza in front of the hotel, and people were dancing. Danielle saw me and called me. She introduced me to her husband, Robert, a very good looking young man in his thirties. I stood there, kind of paralyzed, while she told him that I was the Countess de Roquefeuille's grandchild. He shook my hand and asked me if I wanted to sit down and have a drink with them. I accepted. I ordered a panaché, which is a mixture of beer and lemonade, a very popular beverage in France. Then she said that Robert was not crazy about dancing, and asked me if I would dance with her. I almost fainted... but I could not refuse, as Robert might have wondered why I would not dance with his wife. So we went on the dance floor, holding each other at a distance this time. My legs, my arms, my brain were shaking. We danced a couple of times while Robert smiled at us. Eventually, I had to leave, and bid them both "Bonne nuit." That night, I learned how to keep cool in the face of possible danger!

Danielle and Robert were returning to Paris together a few days later. With anticipation and gratitude in my heart, I went to the hotel to say goodbye. Robert shook my hand in a friendly fashion and got into the car. Danielle kissed me on the cheek and whispered in my ear, "Please never forget me." And she was gone.

So you see, beautiful Danielle, I have never forgotten you!

Chapter 8

From Marseille to Paris

I HAD BEEN admitted to the Université d'Aix-Marseille for my first year of medicine which was called Le PCB (Physics, Chemistry, Biology). My father thought that I would make a good surgeon because I had long and slender fingers; I guess that, in his mind, that was enough to become a famous knife man! He did not mind spending a small fortune so that I could become a doctor—he was eager to see me go through my seven years of medicine.

I rented a room at the Cité Universitaire de Marseille which was then located on Rue Saint Féréol. Every day, I attended the classes. I tried very hard to learn those formulas of chemistry and physics which were so foreign to my mind. My brain was not born to understand these strange juxtapositions of numbers and letters—they looked like Chinese to me. And Physics and Chemistry had not been my forte in school, anyway. Also, after the seven years of Jesuit boarding school, I was not looking forward to another seven years of carving cadavers and witnessing surgeries, with blood spurting out in the nurses' faces. I needed to enjoy my freedom and fly in the fresh air of the big city (yes, the air was still fresh in Marseille in those days!).

I was 18 years old, I was on my own, and it felt like I was in Shangri-La. Two or three times a week, I went with a couple of friends to a little bar near Le Vieux-Port and La Canebière, where pretty young ladies came to chat and hold a glass of Bandol wine. Chez Maurice was the name of that bar, and the owner, Maurice (what a coincidence) played guitar and sang the latest hit songs. One night, I asked him if I could sing a song that was a hit by an American singer, Eddie Constantine, who was an enormous star in France. He said yes. The song started with these lyrics: "On ne m'a pas mis sur terre pour m'tuer à travailler, mais pour vivre à ma manière et goûter à la liberté," which means, "I was not put on this earth to kill myself working, but to live my own way and to taste freedom." How perfect for me. I sang, and everyone in the bar applauded like crazy! Maurice was very happy, and told me that I could come and sing whenever I wanted and my drinks would be complimentary. I was earning free drinks for my songs—I felt like I was already a professional! So I went often to Chez Maurice, not only to sing, but to meet the pretty women who started to be interested in me.

Since the bar was located a couple of blocks from the Marseille Opera, one would think that the area was rather refined, but it was not completely safe because a couple of other bars were frequented by Corsican gangsters who tried to behave well, but sometimes got out of hand. One night, we heard several gunshots just outside Chez Maurice and we did not dare go out for most of the night.

At some point, when everything seemed to have calmed down, I was faced with a little problem. At this time of night, there were no buses and the Cité Universitaire was quite far. I did not know what to do. One of the girls I had been flirting with invited me to her place; it was just a block away. She was beautiful, and I followed her without any hesitation. We went upstairs into her apartment, which was lovely. It was late, so we did not waste any time. We got undressed, lay on the bed, and before we could start anything, she took me in her arms and said: "I must tell you that I am a lesbian. But because I like you, I want to try to see if I can enjoy making love with a man."

It was about 4 in the morning. An hour earlier, I had been scared stiff (in a manner of speaking), and I had drunk more than necessary. I had been ready for a fun night, but suddenly, there she was asking me to represent all of mankind! A tired, scared, half-drunk young man who had just spent seven years in a Jesuit boarding school was being asked by a lesbian to be the Pride of Manhood! The circumstances were not perfect for that endeavor, and I failed miserably. I was always sorry to have missed the opportunity to perhaps make her love men, too. But I am sure that, whatever side of the game she played, she must be a happy lady today.

Needless to say, all that extracurricular activity did not help my studies one bit. The July exam was a disaster. So, I wrote my father that medicine was not made for me, and because my forte had been in literature rather than physics and chemistry, I should study law… in Paris, at La Sorbonne. My father agreed, and I registered at La Sorbonne in the fall. I literally went there once, the first day of the semester. I sat in the amphitheater, listened to the professor, looked around me, and I knew that the law also, was not my cup of coffee. Since Paris was the center of show business in France, that's where one had to be to become a success. I decided that, from then on, I had to concentrate on my singing career.

I found a job as a waiter at the YMCA and took acting lessons with a respected drama teacher, Raymond Girard. These acting classes made me lose my southern accent, and I was now able to play any part, not just the roles of a southerner. There, I met a very funny guy, Michel Conto, who had had a part in a movie; we became very good friends, and still are to this day. But the YMCA job was not enough to make a living, and I went to audition in some cabarets. That's how my career started. My first cabaret was Chez André Pasdoc. I was earning what today would be two dollars a night... the beginning of my fortune!

Then, I auditioned in a second cabaret, where a young rising star was performing. His name was Jacques Brel, and he had already recorded a couple of hits. During my audition, Brel was in the room, and when I finished I heard him say to the lady owner, "Take him, he's got something." WOW! Thanks to Jacques Brel, I was booked at L'Echelle de Jacob, which was then considered a very prestigious cabaret in Paris, in the Saint-Germain-des-Près neighborhood. Now, I was making four dollars a night!

I lived in a tiny room in the attic of an eight floor building without elevators. Climbing eight floors every day kept me in a good shape. My room was really small: it had only one single bed, no night table, no chest of drawers, just one shelf hanging dangerously on the wall. The only place I could anchor my suitcase was at the foot of the bed. There was one bathroom on the floor for all the tenants who were struggling like me. No bath, no shower. But in the next street there were public baths that I could only afford two times a week. It was not the Ritz, and certainly not the kind of show business I had seen in the Hollywood movies!

But there was a big window, without curtains, and each night, I could see the moon winking at me. And that's how I wrote my first song "Madame La Lune," which in English means "Madame The Moon."

Chapter 9

I Am in Show Biz!

I T WAS 1955. I was 20 years old. My songs were being published by Raoul Breton Music Publishing, who also published the works of Charles Trenet, Gilbert Bécaud and Charles Aznavour, the biggest stars in France. I recorded "Madame la Lune" for the French Columbia Record Company, but it went nowhere.

Every night, I sang in a small cabaret, Le Sully de Montmartre, which was located on Place Pigalle, not far from my building. It was not an important cabaret, but I could sing there around 9 p.m., and at 1 or 2 in the morning. It allowed me to pick up a few francs, which I needed badly, since my income was still quite mediocre. Some of the customers in that cabaret were the ladies of the night who came there to have a drink during their breaks. They also came to listen to me. They liked me very much. Every night, we would talk about life in general, and they knew that I was struggling financially. So very often, after my show, they would take turns, and one of them would buy me supper. It was an inspiration for a song that I wrote for them "Les Filles de la Rue" ("The Girls of the Street"). I never forgot the warmth and the kindness of these women who sincerely wanted to help me, no strings attached. I never had an affair with them—their pimps would not have liked it!

One night, by pure chance, a film producer was having dinner at Le Sully de Montmartre with a few friends. I did not know that he was a producer, and I sang my songs as usual. After the show, he invited me to his table. His name was Jean Gourget, and he was preparing a movie about a group of young guys in the South of France. He asked me if I could do a southern accent, and of course I told him that I was from Avignon and that I could speak with a southern accent at anytime. The next day, I went to audition, and got the part—I was really excited! The irony was that I had worked very hard to lose my southern accent, but I had to take it back for my first film! The title of the movie was "Les Promesses Dangereuses" ("The Dangerous Promises"). We shot in the town of Sète in the southwest of the Mediterranean Sea coast. My name was above the title with Rellys, who had been a star in the 1930s and 40s, and Maria Candido, who was a well known singer at that time. The young female star was Françoise Vatel, and the cast included another young actor who was very talented, Roger Dumas, who had a successful career in the theater, TV and movies. It was my first film and I was the star... how lucky could I get?

In 1955, there was still an American base just outside Paris: the Supreme Headquarters Allied Powers Europe (SHAPE). American phonograph records were very difficult to find in Paris then, and when you could, they were very expensive. Also, only affluent people could afford a bottle of scotch. Drinking scotch had become a very fashionable thing to do for the young crowd. A shrewd entrepreneur by the name of Paul Pacini had made a few connections with some American officers from the SHAPE. He knew there was a military commissary that sold everything to the soldiers, from Kleenex to cigarettes to records to... scotch! Through his connections, he was buying the latest records by Sinatra, Bobby Darin, Peggy Lee and others, as well as bottles of scotch (called whisky in France), at a reasonable price. He had some parties in his apartment, and invited his friends and their guests to listen to the music that we were crazy about, and at the same time sell some bottles of whisky. I was lucky enough to have been invited to one of these parties by a friend of his, and the evening was magical. People were dancing on his carpet!

Lo and behold, Paul came up with an idea that revolutionized the nights of Paris. He opened a private club where he could play the records that made people dance, and sell his whisky by the bottle. We would have a glass or two, then keep the bottle in a locked box on the wall. We had our name on the box and our own key to open it, and we could retrieve the bottle every time we came back. And all we had to pay for was a new bottle when the previous one was empty. The walls of the club were covered with a multitude of whisky boxes. So, he named his private club the "Whisky à Gogo" ("à gogo" in French slang means "as much as you want"). And because the English word "record" is "disque" in French, the word "discothèque" was invented. Thanks to Paul Pacini, *discothèques* took over Paris (and the world), and the term "whisky à gogo" became a household name. And through him, I was able to buy the latest American *disques*.

When I got booked at the Echelle de Jacob, I did quite well, and a record company called Vogue signed me. One night, I met a sexy woman and I offered her a drink. Trying to seduce her, I said, "Would you like to come to my place, I have the latest Frank Sinatra album." She laughed and answered, "I do not need Frank Sinatra to go to your place!" We stayed together about two years. Her name was Michelle. She was my first serious relationship.

Then things started to happen. I was appearing in many

cabarets, I was on television, I made several records, and one day my agent sent me on an audition for the well-known French film director, Hervé Bromberger, who was making a film called "Asphalte." And guess what? I got the starring part with Françoise Arnoul, who was a big movie star, and Danny Saval, who became a big star later on. My name was again above the title. In the cast, there was a character actor who was much respected for his great talent. His name was Marcel Bozuffi, who some years later was cast as the killer in the American film "The French Connection."

Starring in "Asphalte" allowed me to buy a little studio in Paris on Boulevard de Clichy, near Place Blanche, which was not yet a bad neighborhood. That little studio was far from being lavish but it was mine, and I was very proud of it.

In those days, France was at war in Algeria. The military service was mandatory and lasted 28 months. When the army called me, I was very upset, as my career was just starting, and 28 months in show business is an eternity. The French Government and the Algerian Rebels were talking in Geneva to find a solution to end the war. Everybody knew that in a matter of three to six months, the war would be over, and I certainly did not want to be sent to the Algerian front to be killed! But I had to go.

First, they sent me to the city of Constance in Germany, on the beautiful Lake Constance, which was the area still under French control, since Germany was still occupied by the Allied Forces as required by the Capitulation document signed by the Germans. There, I did four months of basic training. During that time, the young sergeant in charge of my barracks, who knew that I had starred in a couple of movies, and that my records were being played on the French radio, found his moment of power and targeted me to make my life really miserable. Every day, I had to clean the toilets or wash the floor. And while I was doing it, he and his pals were watching me, and laughing at me. Then, the captain called me into his office and told me that, because of my education, I had the choice of remaining a private or becoming an officer. The army needed officers on the battlefront. The professional officers were trying to avoid going to the fighting line, and therefore were trying to enroll the drafted kids to take their place. They did not want to be killed—and neither did I! So of course, I refused to be an officer. They decided then to make my life even more miserable. So, I had to do something drastic.

For one month, I only ate one apple and a dozen sugar cubes per day, and I drank gallons of coffee so I would not sleep. One of my girlfriends came from Paris to visit me and gave me some pills that kept me awake all night. With that diet, you lose a lot of weight in a month—but I would not recommend it, as I got very sick. So sick, that they had to send me back to the military hospital in Paris called The Val-de-Grace.

I was kept in a secluded area, which was the psychiatric ward. The psychiatrist was very nice, and tried to take good care of me. We talked every day for quite some time, and that's when I learned from him that the other patients in the rooms next to me were the famous designer Yves St. Laurent, the movie star Jacques Charrier (Brigitte Bardot's husband at the time), the song writer Guy Béart (Emmanuelle's father), and the actor Sami Frey—I guess that they were also trying to avoid the war! And we were right, since the Algerian war ended just a few months later!

They kept me in the Val-de Grace for 13 months, so that my "psychiatric problem" could be cured. The day of my release from the hospital, as I was packing my clothes, the doctor came to give me my discharge documents that he signed in front of me, and in a very friendly way wished me good luck in my career. Then, out of nowhere, he said, "Now that you have your papers, you have nothing to worry about. So, you can tell me if you were faking your problem. Because if you were faking it, I must admit that you are a very good actor." I did not expect that; I had to think fast. Even though he had told me on a few occasions that he did not agree with the war, I was not sure if he was serious, or just trying to get me to spill the beans. Since I was still in the hospital, he could stop my release and do who-knows-what. I could not afford to give away my drastic solution that allowed me to do only 17 months in the army instead of 28. I had to continue playing my game. I looked at him with shock in my eyes and softly said, "You are the doctor, and you must know that I was not faking it. I am really surprised by your question. But I want to thank you for helping me with my problem, and for your good wishes." We shook hands, we smiled at each other, and I left the Val-de-Grace with relief in my heart... and with quivering legs! I will never know for sure if I had really convinced him.

It was a dark period in my life, and I am not proud of it. But sometimes, you have to do what you have to do to survive. Unfortunately, that whole episode did not help my career. Indeed, during that time, the New Wave came to dominate the movie industry, and rock and roll took over the music business. So, when I came back, everything I had done before did not count at all. I was 25, and I was a "has been!" Even though I was able to find work in some cabarets, I was unable to transform myself into a rock and roll singer. I could not perform that type of music, but I enjoyed very much watching Johnny Hallyday, the French Elvis Presley. He really was a great stage performer, as well as the darling of French audiences.

CHAPTER 10

Piaf

ONE OF my friends in the business, Félix Marten, was a star in France, as a singer and an actor. He was the French "Saint" on the screen, and recorded many discs. When I knew him, he was having an affair with the legendary Edith Piaf. He was singing one my songs in his show, and liked another one I had written, "La Fille du Port" ("The Girl of the Port"). He thought that Edith might like it, too, and invited me to meet her and sing the song for her in her apartment. So, one evening, I went to her home, and there she was: the great Edith Piaf! She was really petite, and very down to earth. She made me feel very comfortable, and asked me to sing the song Felix had told her about. She seemed to enjoy it, but it was not what she was look-ing for at that moment. She passed on it, but she put her hand on my arm, and in a very affectionate way asked me if I could stay to have dinner with them. Of course, I accepted. It was wonderful to meet this extraordinary lady in person. She had a strong Parisian accent, and loved risqué jokes.

She was very funny, earthy, and unpretentious. Her health at that time was still relatively good. We had a simple dinner at her place, and a couple of shots of cognac with the dessert. At the end of the evening, I thanked Félix, and she gave me a big hug. An evening in Edith Piaf's apartment is not something you forget easily!

The next summer, I was chosen to be part of the French Team that was going to compete in a new contest called "La Coupe d'Europe de la Musique" (The European Cup of Music). Each country had a team of five singers, each one singing in a different style: opera, comic, jazz, etc. I was the "charm" singer. The event took place in Belgium at the Casino of Knokke-Le Zoute, a very elegant and very popular beach resort on the North Sea. The Casino was a magnificent building in the turn of the century style.

It was summertime, and the air was warm and cheerful. We sang every night, and every night, one team was eliminated. The last two teams remaining in the finals were France and England. I thought that England would win—they had a singer who not only was a very beautiful girl but also a very talented jazz singer. I really loved listening to her. But France won, and we were proud to have won!

The next night, Edith Piaf was giving a concert in the big casino showroom. She had come one day early with her conductor, to have enough time to rehearse with the orchestra. That night she attended the finals, and saw us perform. She came backstage to compliment us. She was very happy that France had won, and we took pictures with her. I still have one that I cherish. But she did not remember that I had dinner with her and Félix in her apartment in Paris.

After the show, the beautiful English girl, the jazz singer, approached me and started speaking to me in the language of Shakespeare. I had learned English in school, but I could not really converse fluently; I could only understand and mumble some simple words. I said, "Sorrrry, me no underrrstand verrry

With Edith Piaf and the French team that won the
Grand Prix de la Chanson in Knokke-le-Zoute,
Belgium, 1960

well." She said, "It's okay — congratulations." I answered, "I underrrstand congrrratulations, sank you verrry much." She smiled a very sexy smile, and I continued, "I love you sing." She laughed and said, "I love you sing, too!" We knew then that the language was not important. We were two young creatures appreciating each other in that moment in time. We had one last night to kill... and, as they say, what happens in Knocke-Le-Zoute stays in Knocke-Le-Zoute!

About a year later, I had the experience of a lifetime with Edith Piaf. In those days in France, during the summer, different kinds of variety shows were presented in all the vacation spots that had casinos or theaters. Stars would appear one night only in each city. It was the era of the music hall shows, with a first half that consisted of two or three acts performing before the second half that belonged to the star. My agent called me one day to tell me that he had booked me in a show with the great Edith Piaf! The gala was to be held at the old Palais des Festivals in Cannes, where the famous Cannes Festival used to show the selected movies every year in May. That old Palais des Festivals no longer exists today. But then, great stars appeared there between July and September, when all the French are on vacation. I was booked to close the first half, just before Edith Piaf's performance. To say that I was thrilled is an understatement—I was in heaven!

By now, Edith was not in a good health and needed a lot of care. On the night of the show, I performed my songs, and decided to stay in the wings for the second half, to enjoy the talent of that legend, and to learn. The curtains were down. And suddenly, there she was: so tiny, so frail, so vulnerable. She could hardly walk; two men were holding her. They helped position her so she could lean against the piano with her two hands behind her back while holding the piano. I wondered how she would be able to do her show.

When the orchestra began playing a medley of her hits, the audience started to applaud. In the pop category, it was classical music. It was a long medley, and when it started to fade out, the curtains slowly rose. The audience stood up, cheering for several minutes, and that's when the miracle happened. This petite lady, who just a moment ago looked like she was going to faint, left the piano, walked to the edge of the stage, her head up and her arms opened to the public, and started to sing as if nothing was wrong. I could not believe it. Her voice was hypnotic. She sang for almost an hour under the ovation of an adoring crowd that was electrified and transported to the height of euphoria. The love from the audience embraced her whole being, enveloping her heart and making her feel alive. I realized that her life was about touching the audience that brought her pure joy in return. It was a unique phenomenon that I would never experience again. When the show ended, even though the acclamations did not stop, the curtains slowly came down. She staggered back towards the piano, and the two men rushed to her side. They grasped her arms to help her walk. As she was passing by me, I said "You were marvelous tonight, Edith, thank you." She looked at me. Her eyes were hesitant. She struggled to give me a smile. I thought she wanted to say something, but she did not have the strength. Without a word, she vanished into her dressing room. It was my last vision of Edith Piaf, and I still have goose-pimples just remembering it. It was a spectacular event, and a memory that will be with me until the rest of my days.

Unfortunately, it became more and more difficult for me to find work. I started to think very seriously of quitting the business.

CHAPTER 11

First Cruise

A ND THEN, a strange thing happened. The transatlantic ship Le Liberté was looking for a singer to entertain the passengers during her last trip to the USA, and my agent signed me for the job. At the time, singing on a ship was not a job to be proud of—no star would even think of it! And I was a little ashamed of having to do it. But my financial situation was rather bleak, and I had to accept it. And the idea of a round trip to New York was kind of fulfilling my dreams of Hollywood and my adventurous spirit.

One morning, I took the train to the harbor in Le Havre where Le Liberté was anchored, and I boarded the ship. The cruise director welcomed me warmly. He remembered me from the films I had made three or four years before, and from my records that were played on the radio. He gave me a first class cabin which was really beautiful.

We left Le Havre in the evening for our first and only port of call, Southampton, England. We arrived the next morning to pick up more passengers, mostly Americans. The Cruise Director and I were watching the people coming on board when a very attractive and elegant woman passed in front of us. She must have been about 30 years old. I said to the Cruise Director, "What a pretty lady!" He said, "Don't even think about it. She is English, and she is married to the Chairman of the Board of a large American corporation. And that's her little boy with the nanny behind her." I said that I was only making an observation, and that I would never dare try anything with such a lady. A few hours later, we embraced the open sea on our way to New York.

The journey was wonderful. In the first class restaurant, I had my own table and I became friendly with the four *garçons* who were in charge of my table. In those days, the service was extraordinary: one sommelier, one Chef de Table and two waiters were assigned to serve me. Of course, each table received the same astounding service. The food, the caviar, the foie gras, the wines, the champagne were all heavenly! Suddenly, I was no longer ashamed of having signed this contract. But, of course, I was there to sing. I did two shows, and the reaction from the American crowd was amazing. They loved me!

After my first show, an American gentleman invited me to his table and introduced me to his guests. Among them was the lady I had seen coming on board. At some point, every one was dancing, and I found myself alone at the table with the lady. To be polite, I invited her to dance; it was a slow dance. There she was in my arms, but I had no sexual intentions whatsoever... I was just trying to be social. During our dance, I was trying to say a few words in my poor English. She smiled and told me that she spoke French. What a relief! At the end of the dance, we went back to the table and conversed in French.

When the band stopped playing, we followed her friends to the upper deck where a piano player was playing in a small bar for the late crowd. We had a drink, and listened to the piano player who was quite good. Little by little, everyone left the bar to get back to their cabins, and she asked me to accompany her to hers. On the way, she held my arm. The corridor was completely empty, and the only noise was the constant whisper of the ship engine. I really don't know how it happened, but as we were saying good night, we kissed, and we kissed, and she opened her door and closed it behind us. She said, "I don't know what's coming over me. I have never done anything like this... but suddenly, the idea of a shipboard romance really appeals to me." Remembering what the Cruise Director had told me, I was a little hesitant. But there in my arms was a lovely lady, a very beautiful one, a very sophisticated one, who was asking for help. What's a man supposed to do? I just could not refuse her and make her feel bad, especially since that shipboard romance appealed to me, too!

So, we let ourselves go, and spent part of the night together. At around 4 a.m., she very cautiously let me out. We repeated the dangerous adventure once more. I had to be very careful. I knew that she really was a lady. That adventure was just one of those things.

The day before we arrived in New York, a very distinguished couple named Mr. and Mrs. Campbell came to me and told me that if I ever wanted to sing in New York, they could help me because, even though they were not in show business, they knew a few people who were. With my broken English, I thanked them, and they gave me their business card.

The next morning, I got up at 5. I did not want to miss our entry into the Port of New York. I climbed up to the upper deck. Through the mist, I could see the millions of lights of Manhattan. It was a surrealist painting, a surreal world, a mysterious world, a new world. And suddenly there she was—

the Statue of Liberty! It is difficult to describe the emotion that a young man, born in Ethiopia, could feel in such a moment. I knew that she was French, so, as we were sailing by her, I said, "Bonjour Madame, vous êtes très belle." I swear that she winked at me and whispered, "Bienvenue à New York!" This was not a movie... I was really there.

After we docked and the passengers started to disembark, I saw the lady leaving with her son and the nanny. She glanced at me, smiled, and disappeared...

Later on, I went ashore, jumped in a taxi and told the cabbie, "Rockefeller Center, please." He took me there, and I paid and got out of the cab. Slowly, my eyes looked up, and up, and up... I had never seen such a building. I was mesmerized. There I was, on Fifth Avenue! St. Patrick's Cathedral looked so small next to the skyscrapers. And then, there I was on Park Avenue, the Waldorf Astoria in front of me! I kept walking and looking at the street signs, and suddenly I saw Broadway! A large sign above a gate said, "Fred Astaire Dance Studio." I could not believe my eyes. It was magic. I really was in the new world!

A friend of mine from Paris was in the cast of a French Revue called "La Plume de Ma Tante" ("My Aunt's Pen"). I went to the artists' entrance and asked for him. We met after the show over a drink in some club he knew. We talked about Paris, we talked about Broadway, we talked about how lucky we were to be in this business. It was about 3 a.m. when I got back to the ship. I had fallen in love with New York, and I was exhausted. I fell asleep with a smile on my face.

The next day, we sailed back to Europe. Five days later, we docked in Southampton, England, and on the sixth day, we ended that transatlantic adventure in Le Havre, where I would take a train back to Paris. What I remember about that return trip is that among the passengers was a big movie star whom I had seen in several films. His name was Ernie Kovacs. He did a show one night for the passengers, and he was hysterical. His beautiful wife Edie Adams was with him. After my first show, I had the pleasure of shaking hands with them, and also with a young lady who was a regular on the American TV show, "The Garry Moore Show." Her name was Carol Burnett. She and I, with a few other passengers, were invited to dine at the captain's table one evening. This was an honor. I did not understand everything she said, but I understood that she was a very funny lady, and I enjoyed her very much.

CHAPTER 12

New York

B ACK IN Paris, I was cleaning my desk one day, and I found the business card that the American couple had given me on Le Liberté. I wrote them a letter asking if they really could help me meeting some show biz people, and they answered yes. Now, I was faced with a very serious decision that would determine the rest of my life. I talked with my friends, with my agent, and I even consulted a tarot card reader! Finally, I realized that, since I was a "has-been" in Paris, I had to take a chance to be a new face in a new country, especially a country called America. It had been my dream since I was a little boy, and now I had the chance to make that dream a reality. And of course, my adventurous spirit was telling me, "Marco Polo did not hesitate to go to China, Henry Morton Stanley did not hesitate to presume exploring Central Africa and find Dr. Livingstone, Christopher Columbus did not hesitate to sail west to discover America, even though he thought that it was Asia, and in fact he only landed in The Bahamas... so it is your turn to discover the United States, even though it is already full of skyscrapers and world-renowned movie stars! Do not hesitate to go west, young man!" That was a convincing argument. So, I said to myself, "Why not?"

It took some time to organize the official papers—passport,

working visa, airplane tickets—and to set up meetings in New York. I had to take English lessons at Berlitz so I could somehow communicate with the first Americans I would meet. Many other details had to be taken care of ahead of such an important move, ahead of such a radical change of life. I sold my little studio, my car, and put together enough money for me to survive for at least six months, since my first visa was only valid for that long.

And one morning, my friends took me to the Orly Airport. After a few hugs, a few tears, and lots of encouragements, my friends put me on the plane. My heart was jumping with apprehension. I was really diving into the unknown. But I was 27 years old, and I had confidence in my talent, and in my masculine intuition.

The plane landed in New York on January 29, the day before my birthday. The Campbells had rented a cute studio for me on East 52nd street, and it was going to be my nest for the next couple of years.

Of course, I did not know anyone in New York except for the Campbell's friends, who were not of my generation. The Brasserie was an all-night restaurant on East 53rd street. I had been there a few times, and had met the manager, who was from Belgium and spoke perfect French. Through him, I met some young Americans, and one night he introduced me to two attractive girls who were amused by my French accent— especially one of them, who volunteered to teach me English, and invited me to her apartment. (Let me interpolate here that I had arrived about three months before that evening, and I had had no chance of meeting anyone of the opposite sex... so, certain needs of the young man I was had not been fulfilled!).

I accepted her invitation wholeheartedly. When we got there, she tried to teach me some new words, but one thing led to another, and eventually we found ourselves naked in her bed. She wanted to prove that American women were as good as French women as lovers, and she succeeded. When she reached her pinnacle, she screamed, "Vive la France!" I smiled and started singing "La Marseillaise!" She laughed, then concentrated on the job at hand. She did very well... and, when my turn came, she yelled "Welcome to America!" I could not stop laughing! Eventually, we went to sleep. When I left her place, I knew that my decision to come to America was a very good one. I never saw that gracious lady again, but she left in my heart a lasting memory.

Now, I had to really try to learn how to speak better English. Every day, I took with me a piece of paper and a pen, and wrote down every word I did not know that I would see on a wall, on a bus, on a taxi, in a window, anywhere. Back in my apartment, I would find their meaning in my dictionary and memorize them. But that would not teach me the pronunciation of these words. By chance, one afternoon, I was watching TV and saw a game show called Password; the host was Allen Ludden. The game consisted of two celebrities sitting down with one contestant each. Unknown to the contestants, a word was displayed on the bottom of the screen, and a voice that the contestants could not hear was enunciating that word for the TV viewers. The celebrity received a note with the word on it, and had to make the contestant find out what was that word by means of synonyms. So, there I was, hearing the pronunciation of the word and learning its meaning through synonyms. That game helped me a lot with my English, and I am sorry that I never had a chance to meet Mr. Ludden to thank him for that fun and free English lesson!

Mr. Campbell introduced me to a personal manager who obtained an audition for me at the Blue Angel, a prestigious cabaret of New York, where people such as Barbara Streisand appeared when they started in the business. A couple of weeks later, I learned that my audition was successful, and that I was booked to open the show for a young stand-up comedian who then was only well known in New York. His name? Woody Allen!

Two songwriters, Lyn Duddy and Jerry Bresler, helped me with my act, and wrote a song that I loved and that I have never stopped singing through my career: "Vive La Difference." The first line of the song is: "You've got lips, I've got lips, the possibilities are simply immense, cause you're a girl and I'm a boy, Oh, la, la and vive la difference!" Lyn and Jerry certainly hit it on the lips!

I had met Jean-Pierre Aumont in France where he was a big movie star as well as in the States. He happened to be in New York rehearsing a Broadway musical with the beautiful legend Vivien Leigh, whose famous last words of "Gone With The Wind," "Tomorrow is another day" will be forever engraved in the memory of cinema aficionados. Jean-Pierre was there the night of my premiere at the Blue Angel. Vivien was rehearsing that evening and could not come, but Jean-Pierre brought a couple of his friends. One was another legend of the movie world, Gloria Swanson, and the other was Johnny Ray whose record "Cry" had been a phenomenal success. Was I nervous? No... I was petrified!

My show went very well, and I stayed backstage to listen to Woody Allen. My English was still rusty, and I could not

My opening night at the Blue Angel,
with Gloria Swanson and Jean-Pierre Aumont

understand everything, but I could feel that this man was a very special talent.

After the show, Gloria Swanson and Jean-Pierre came to my dressing room to congratulate me, and Miss Swanson decided that my hair was too long, and that she was going to cut it. So, she invited everyone for a drink at her place. Once there, she placed some newspapers on the floor, sat me down on a chair, put a towel around my neck, and... cut my hair! That's one of my most cherished claims to fame: that Gloria Swanson cut my hair in the middle of her living room!

While I was appearing at the Blue Angel, I had a French girlfriend who was a model. One night, she brought her hairdresser to the show. He was very impressed. A few days later, I was in my manager's office when his phone rang. He answered it, listened, and said, "Yes, of course!" He covered the phone with his hand and whispered to me, "Ed Sullivan is calling!"

Then he continued, "Yes Mr. Sullivan, of course, we'll be there."

(Note for younger readers: "The Ed Sullivan Show" was the biggest variety show on TV, with an average of 42 million people watching every Sunday night at 8 p.m.)

When my manager hung up the phone, he turned to me and said, "Your girlfriend's hairdresser is also Mrs. Sullivan's hairdresser. He told her that you were the new Maurice Chevalier. Mrs. Sullivan told her husband that he should look into it. So, Ed found out that I am your manager, and he wants you to audition in front of a live audience during the dress rehearsal next Sunday afternoon." On that particular show, there was an English group called Herman's Hermits, and for the dress rehearsal the theater was full of teenagers. I sang a song called the French Twist, and the kids screamed and gave me an unbelievable reception. Ed Sullivan was really surprised. He shook my hand and complimented me with a great smile. I could feel that he really liked me. And that's how I was signed to appear on eight Ed Sullivan Shows... which gives credence to the old saying, "Only your hairdresser knows for sure!"

On one of my first appearances, I was singing "Standing on the Corner," and the set decorator had built on the stage big cubes of different heights. I had to jump from one to the other during my song. The act before me was the comedian Nipsey Russell, and at the dress rehearsal in the afternoon, when he finished his act, Ed shook his hand, thanked him, and Nipsey left the stage. I knew then that Ed was introducing me, and that's when the orchestra started my intro.

For the live show that evening, I was behind the big cubes looking at the monitor, waiting for Nipsey to leave. I could not hear the dialog, and Nipsey was not leaving. Suddenly, I heard that the orchestra had started the intro of my arrangement, and that the camera was on me. I was very confused and I could not start singing. So Ed came behind the camera and said, "We are going to start again." The band stopped, restarted my musical intro, and I was able to sing at last. That's when the audience started applauding to help me. I really don't know how I finished

My first appearance on the
Ed Sullivan Show, 1964

the song. I had no idea how I did perform, but when I looked at the video some time later, it did not show that I was shaking deep in my belly! I was the last performer on that particular show, and Ed came quickly to shake my hand, put his arms around my shoulders and said good night. The curtain was down, and I was so ashamed that I remained on the stage, sitting on one of the set pieces. Ed came to me and said, "Don't worry. I liked it because it reminded people that this is a live show. Everything is fine." I still could not put myself together, and then another performer on the show came to me, embraced me and gave me a big kiss. The performer was Juliet Prowse! That made me feel better right away, and I finally went to my dressing room and picked myself up. Then, I learned what had happened. The show was running late, so Ed asked Nipsey Russell to stay with him to listen to Jean-Paul Vignon, but I did not hear that, and that was the reason for my confusion.

The next day, I was walking on Fifth Avenue by myself, and a guy came to me, looked at me, and said, "Aren't you the guy who fucked up on The Ed Sullivan Show last night?" I could only say, "Yes, I am the one!"

Another memorable show with Ed was when they decided to have me sing a duet with an 18-year-old girl who was starting to make a name for herself. Her mother was Judy Garland, and (of course) she was Liza Minnelli. We were performing one of Charles Trenet's songs, "Boum." It was January, and the weather was quite cold. We rehearsed during the week, wrapped up in thick and warm sweaters which did not make it easy to dance the fun moves that the choreographer had created for the two of us. Liza was adorable and very professional. Sunday came, we performed the duet, and it was a big success. That performance did not age, and is still enjoyable today.

That's when Columbia Records signed me. My first single made it to number 38 in the Billboard charts. The song was "Don't Cry Little Girl." It had teen-age appeal, but never climbed to number one.

There was one song I was doing in my act that was a big hit in France, but not yet known in the U.S. I was singing it half in

*My duet with Liza Minnelli
on the Ed Sullivan Show, 1965*

French and half in English, and the audience always received it with thunderous applause. I wanted to record that song, but the people in charge at Columbia thought that it was a good song on the stage, but not good recording material. So, I did not record it in my first album, "Because I Love You." But after I had recorded the album, Herb Alpert released an instrumental version of that song; it shot to number one in the charts, and Sonny & Cher also recorded the song with great success. That's when Columbia decided that I should record a single of it… but it was too late. The song was "Et Maintenant," known in English as "What Now My Love." But that's show biz!

In order to promote my album, Columbia sent me on a tour around the country. What I remember most was the stop in

Los Angeles. My agency and Columbia had organized a special party for the media at the Beverly Hills Hotel. It was hosted by two young actresses who were already making a big name for themselves, Suzanne Pleshette and Connie Stevens. A brunette and a blonde, both absolutely gorgeous! I sang my song "Vive La Difference" to them, and they were really sweet.

I stayed at the Beverly Hills Hotel for about four days. One day, I was lounging by the pool, talking business with my agent. On the other side of the pool, just across from us, were several cabanas, rented on a regular basis to wealthy customers. Since cell phones did not exist then, there were phone plugs around the pool and when a call came, the waiter would bring a phone and just plug it in.

Except for my agent, no one really knew me then. That's why I was surprised when the waiter came with a phone and told me, "A call for you, sir." Who would call me here? I picked up the receiver and said, "Allo?" A feminine voice answered, "Look across the pool in cabana number four. I am the girl with long blond hair, and I am waving at you. Do you see me?" I looked, and saw a very attractive young woman in a bikini. I said, "I see you. What can I do for you?" She said, "In half an hour, I will be in my room. Number 304. I'll be waiting for you." And she hung up. As she was leaving her cabana, my eyes instinctively followed her. She had a sensuous body and her walk was very flirtatious, a little like Mae West used to walk! I turned to my agent to tell him what had just happened. He started laughing, could not stop laughing, and said, "I have to be at the office in half an hour. I'll call you later. Now, go enjoy yourself!"

I was really curious. Half an hour later, I was knocking on her door. She opened it. She was wearing a very sexy negligee.

She smiled, took my hand, guided me to the bed, dropped her negligee and undressed me. She was quite hungry. We made love for about an hour. She got dressed, I got dressed, and with a warm smile, she guided me to the door, opened it, and let me out. During the whole interlude, not one word was exchanged. I never knew her name, or where she was living. I never had such a robotic experience again, but I certainly never forgot that one... thank you Gloria Steinem!

A few weeks later, I was booked on "The Red Skelton Comedy Hour," a network television show. I had seen Red Skelton in a movie with Esther Williams, and thought he was very funny. I was so excited to be singing, and even dancing, on his show. During the week, we rehearsed my song with the David Rose Orchestra, a fantastic big band of that era with a whole rhythm section, five saxophones, four trumpets, four trombones—I was in heaven. Then, the choreographer guided my dancing with eight beautiful girls who liked my French accent, and one in particular who giggled each time I opened my mouth.

On the day of the taping, I was getting ready in my dressing room, when I heard a knock on the door. I opened it, and standing right there in front of me was Red Skelton himself. He smiled, and in a kind of shy way said, "Hi, my name is Red Skelton, and I wanted to welcome you to the show." I mumbled, "Thank you," and he left. A big star like him took the time to welcome me in person. What a great lesson for me! I did the show, and he thanked me with great affection.

After that, I made several appearances on the "Tonight Show with Johnny Carson," and became a regular guest on the "Merv Griffin Show." Merv, his wife Julann, and their son Anthony, liked me; they invited me several times to have dinner in their home. We became friends. In fact, when I got married, Merv and Julann were the only guests who were not "family."

On one of Merv's shows, the fabulous Greer Garson was one of his guests. I was thrilled. I had a crush on her when I was a teenager, after seeing her in the movies "Mrs. Miniver" and "Madame Curie." Before the show, I had told Merv something quite naughty that had just happened to me. He asked me to repeat the story on the show, because he liked when I said something risqué—it spiced up the show, and I could get away with it because I was French! So, I told the following story: "A good friend of mine, Eric, who was a womanizer and had several girl friends, told me that one of his girls found me sexy, and since her birthday was coming up, he would like me to be her birthday gift. But, putting first things first, I wanted to find out who was the lucky girl! When I realized she was quite attractive, I accepted. Eric arranged the whole affair, telling her that she would find her present at a certain address. She did not know that it was my address, and had no idea what she would find there. On the night and time agreed upon, she knocked on my door. I opened it. She could not believe it. She was shocked, but she played the game. It was a good game, and she was a good player. I wished her a happy birthday! In the morning, she called Eric to thank him before she left my place." Merv loved that story!

When the show was over, I went up to Greer Garson, kissed her hand and told her that I was a big fan, and that it had been an honor to meet her. She thanked me, and as she was leaving, she turned around and said in her classy English accent, "By the way, Jean-Paul, my birthday is next week!" She smiled, and walked away gracefully. That was another anecdote that never left my mind!

CHAPTER 13

Chevalier

DURING this time, there was a popular talk show on a New York radio station. Regretfully, I cannot recall the name of the very popular host. He called me one evening to inform me that he had just interviewed Maurice Chevalier, who said on the air that he had seen me on the Ed Sullivan Show, and his comments were extremely complimentary. "He said that your style, and the way you perform, should appeal to the American audiences, and that you could be the one who would replace him in their hearts. Do you want a copy of the tape of that interview?"

I said, "Yes, of course," and he sent it to me the next day. I blushed when I listened to it; I could not believe how laudatory Chevalier was. Now, I had to try to meet him.

Through my agent, I got his address in France, and wrote him a letter to thank him for his compliments. He wrote back to me, saying that we should meet on his next trip to New York. He contacted me about a year later, and we made an appointment in a French restaurant, of course. I brought with me the lady I was engaged to, whose name was Brigid. He was extremely charming, and we spoke about France, America, and mostly about the business. When the check came, he let me pay without even trying to pick it up... but it was worth it. A few months later, he was going to be the Master of Ceremonies for

Maurice Chevalier introducing me at the Charity
Ball "April in Paris" at the Waldorf Astoria, 1968

an annual charity ball which was a big deal at the time: The
April In Paris Ball at the Waldorf-Astoria Hotel. The organizers
had booked an unknown lady singer from France, but Maurice
insisted on getting me on the show, and made sure that I would
close the show. He introduced me with his arm around my
shoulders, and the audience was very impressed. Thanks to
Maurice, I was a big success. All the French press was there,
right in front of me, and witnessed the audience reception. But
for some unknown reason that I still can not explain, not one
French newspaper present that evening mentioned my name.
Well, that's the way it goes!

While I am talking about my experience with Maurice
Chevalier, I must interject a correction regarding what happened to him during World War II, since there are still people

who believe that Chevalier was a Nazi sympathizer. This is completely false. The commission looking for the Nazi collaborators after the war had targeted him and went through his case thoroughly. Finally, it was proven without any doubt, that he had been wrongly incriminated. I do not think that the real story was reported in the American media, and if it was, it seems nobody paid any attention. So, after researching it myself, here is what Chevalier told me:

The Germans invaded France in 1940 and occupied Paris. In spite of their confusion and humiliation, the Parisians tried to continue living their life. They were going out to restaurants, they were going to the market buying food, clothes, furniture and the other things they needed to survive. They were also going to the theater to try to forget the horrible conditions of the war for a couple of hours. Like many other actors and singers, Maurice Chevalier continued working, and was appearing in the Théatre de l'ABC in Paris. Of course, among the spectators were some German officers and soldiers who were part of the occupation. He had to make a living, and could not refuse to sing just because some Germans were in the audience. His girlfriend was a young singer, Nita Raya, who was Jewish. One night after the show, some German officers went to his dressing room and asked him to do a show in Berlin. Chevalier refused. One of the officers said, "We know that your girlfriend is Jewish. If you want to keep her and her parents in Paris, you should accept our offer." Maurice did not know then about the concentration camps, but realized that it could be a serious problem for Nita and her family. He contacted a representative of the Vichy government which was collaborating with Germany, and made a deal with them: he would sing for the French prisoners in Altengrabow, the camp where he had been himself a prisoner during World War I. In exchange, he demanded the release of ten French prisoners whom he himself would bring back to Paris. He did not get paid; but in November 1941, he sang in front of 3000 prisoners in Altengrabow, and the next day, he brought back the ten prisoners to the acclamation of the Parisians.

In those days, the Germans owned the airwaves, and they were very happy to broadcast that Chevalier had sung in Germany, without giving the details. In London, the Free French under General de Gaulle believed what they heard on the radio, and denounced Maurice Chevalier as a traitor. Back in France, Maurice had discreetly obtained false papers for Nita and her parents, and made them leave Paris in a hurry. He hid them in a farm in Ardèche, which was a poor region located in the bottom half of France that was not occupied by the Germans. He retired to his villa in Cannes, which was also not under Nazi occupation. His villa became an official mailbox for the fighters of the local Resistance, Le Maquis, who controlled the Provence region.

One day, Chevalier thought it would be safe enough to go visit Nita in her hiding place. He took his car and drove toward Ardèche. On the way, just before he got to the farm, some Resistance fighters of that region recognized him and arrested him. All they knew was what they had also heard on the radio: that he sang in Germany, and was therefore a collaborator. He tried to explain what really happened, and told them that he was involved with the Maquis in Provence—to no avail. He asked them to get in touch with the Resistance in Cannes, but communications were very difficult then. He gave them a lot of money to send someone by train to Cannes to find out the truth. They agreed to that; they sent one guy to Cannes, and gave him one week to contact the names that Maurice had given them. One week later, the guy was not back, and they thought that Maurice had lied to them. They were losing their patience.

The next day, they put Chevalier against a wall in the court-yard, tied his hands, put a blindfold over his eyes, and started making fun of him. They were ready to shoot him dead, when the miracle happened: the guy came back from Cannes and stopped the fusillade, just in time. Maurice was cleared, and some very embarrassed young resistance fighters apologized profusely. A very shaky Maurice was released and driven to the farm where Nita was hiding, and he spent a blissful night with her.

Later, when the commission was going through his case, several stars came to Chevalier's defense, among them Marlène Dietrich, as well as intellectuals such as Louis Aragon. But the supreme proof of his innocence came when General Charles de Gaulle, who was then the President of France, invited him to lunch at the Elysée Palace.

I kept in touch with Maurice Chevalier. We exchanged letters and Christmas cards. He was not working very much any more, and stayed in his beloved house in Paris that he had named La Louque, as an homage to his mother's nickname.

One day in 1972, I heard in the news that he had passed away. I felt a deep pain. One of the greatest entertainers of the 20th century was gone; the fact that I had known him personally deepened my sorrow. His unmistakable voice and style were beloved all over the world, and had made him the best ambassador of France. It was a great loss, and the end of an era in show business. He was 84.

Now, I was hoping that it could be the beginning of my era.

Everything was going fine; I had started to make a name for myself. And that's when The Beatles arrived. The music business was almost immediately transformed. Rock and roll, especially performed by self-contained groups, slowly but surely took over the whole industry. I was still a crooner, but the taste of the young public was changing rapidly, and I found myself unable to get a hit record. But I was still appearing on TV and in night clubs around the country.

CHAPTER 14

Brigid

M Y FIRST engagement in Chicago was at the Drake Hotel, in a charming nightclub named The Camellia House. On my opening night, several journalists had been invited, and among them was a famous columnist by the name of Maggie Daly. She asked me to join her table after the show. Maggie's daughter Brigid and Brigid's boyfriend were also there. Maggie was delightful and quite funny. We talked for a long time, but her daughter ignored me completely.

A couple of days later, Maggie invited me to an afternoon party she was giving in her apartment on Lake Shore Drive. I rang the bell, and Brigid opened the door. I had not had a chance to really look at her at the Camellia House, but when she opened the door, I was captivated by her beauty. Her eyes were extraordinary; their color was a combination of blue, green and hazel that made the sky and Lake Michigan very jealous! Her long black hair framed a delicate and pretty face whose pale complexion gave her an air of vulnerability. I said, "Good afternoon, my name is... " and she interrupted me with, "I know what your name is, please come in... and by the way, my name is Brigid Bazlen." She was very charming during the party, asking me many questions about my life. I did the same, and learned that she had been under contract to MGM when she was 16, and that in her first film "The Honeymoon Machine," she starred opposite Steve McQueen—WOW! She also portrayed Salome in the biblical film "The King of Kings." I was impressed. At some point, I asked her: "Where is your boyfriend?" She answered, "Who knows? He was not the kind of man I was looking for." Curious, I inquired, "What kind of man *are* you looking for?" She said, "When I find him, I'll tell you." Then she informed me that she was living in New York, and she was here just to visit her mother. I invited her to have dinner with me on my day off. She accepted.

When my engagement at The Drake ended, I went back to New York and saw Brigid again. Autumn in New York has inspired many poets, and can be very romantic. Hand in hand, we went strolling in Central Park several times. The leaves on the trees had taken too much sun during the long hot summer, and they were suntanned to a crisp. Their range of color was glorious, wavering from pale yellow, to chocolate brown, to devilish red. Gershwin was in the air, with Irving Berlin, Cole Porter, Rogers and Hart, and so many others. The wind played their music, and the autumn leaves were dancing to it. We also went to the theater. The glitter of Broadway was hypnotic. The shows made us jump with joy. We spent many evenings in quaint little restaurants. We were not hungry for food, but the evenings brought us closer. One day, she saw a puppy, a very cute Yorkie, in the window of a pet shop, and she was crazy about it, so I bought it for her. We named her Bijou.

Well... we fell in love. Brigid was 21 years old, and I was 31. I had been thinking seriously about settling down, if I could find the right woman. Brigid seemed to be the one. Beyond the fact that she was beautiful, there was an air of mystery within her femininity which I found intriguing, she had a quirky sense of humor that fascinated me, she had an independent mind, a mind of her own which was definitely challenging, and she was oozing with sensuality. Also, I thought that if I wanted to have a child, I should not wait too long. One day, she asked me for an autographed picture. The confirmed bachelor wrote on it, "Would you marry me?" She giggled, and said yes!

We planned our wedding for April 27 of the following year. My parents were now retired and living in Nice, France. I sent them two tickets so they could come to New York for the big event. I had reserved a suite for them at The New York Drake Hotel. I was financially secure, and I wanted to surprise my mother with something special. I bought her a mink coat, which had been her dream for a very long time. Brigid gave me an idea: instead of giving it to her right away, we hid it, inside out, in the wastepaper basket of their hotel suite. I picked them up at the airport in a limo, and when we arrived at the hotel, we went up to the suite. Our friends had sent gorgeous flower arrangements; the suite was inundated with blossoms of every color. My mother was very touched—she was also really impressed by the fact that there were two TVs, one in the living room and one in the bedroom, unheard of in Nice at the time!

At some point, we were walking past the wastepaper basket, and I said to her, "Look, *maman*, look at what these Americans throw away." She did not understand. I repeated, "Look, look in the basket, can you believe what people throw away in this country?" She was still confused. I said, "Pull that thing out of the basket." She did. As she unfolded the coat, she saw her name sewn in the inside lining. She was now holding the mink coat in amazement. She looked at me, took me in her arms and cried.

Maggie had arranged for the wedding dinner to be held at the 21 Club. The guests were only the members of our family—mostly hers—with the exception of Merv and Julann Griffin, who had become very close to Brigid and me. The reception was beautiful, and the food was delicious. After dessert, each guest gave a little speech with complimentary words about Brigid and me. When my father's turn came, he apologized for not speaking English. He had not understood one word of what everybody else had said, but he had a few words in French... and he sang his famous "Ragazinella" just for me—he was a big hit!

And I was now a married man!

I pause here to recount a little story about Merv and his wife Julann. They really liked my parents, and they invited us to spend the weekend in their beautiful country house outside

With my father, my mother,
and my wife Brigid Bazlen, 1966

New York. It was a great house built on the side of a little river, with a big wheel in the back of the house, turning to the rhythm of the current—the kind of wheel we see on the back of the riverboats that sail on the Mississippi... a very picturesque and elegant home. Julann had two sisters, and when they were younger, they had formed a singing trio that became very popular. But when Julann married Merv, the sisters got out of show business. The first evening we were at Merv and Julann's house, the three sisters sang a couple of songs for my parents, who could not believe how good they were. Brigid and I were also very impressed. Of course, when they were singing, the piano player was Merv!

I had told Julann that my mother was a good cook, and the next day, they decided to cook something together. I was with Merv and Brigid in the family room, when Julann suddenly came to me, apologizing because my mother thought that her cooking was terrible. I could not believe that my mother would say something like that. I went to the kitchen and asked her what was wrong. She said nothing is wrong, everything is terrible! And I started laughing, understanding that there was a language problem. In French, when you say something is *terrible*, it means fabulous. So my mother was telling Julann that everything was fabulous, but in English, terrible does not mean fabulous, and Julann misunderstood the compliment. When I explained the mistake, everyone started laughing... and the dinner was delicious.

At first, Brigid was living in her apartment and I was living in mine, since we had not been able to find one that we both liked. When I told that story on the Merv Griffin show, it created a controversy. It was unthinkable in those days that a husband

and his wife would live separately. America was still a very puritanical country! And every time I was on the show, Merv would ask me, "Still living in different places? Are you still married?" It became a running joke.

Tribute to Maurice Chevalier on the Merv Griffin Show, 1973

Well, it took some time, but we finally found a beautiful home on Park Avenue at 86th Street. Merv's audience was relieved, and our life was wonderful. Especially when Brigid told me that she was pregnant!

I was now a father to be!

A few days later, my agent asked me to fly to Los Angeles to audition for a part in a big movie starring William Holden. Wow—William Holden! I had seen "Sunset Boulevard" and "Picnic" in France, and I was really thrilled! I flew to LA, auditioned for the director, Andrew McLaglen, and the producer David Wolper—and I got the part. The film was "The Devil's

Brigade." In March of 1967, we started shooting in Utah, where we would stay for a couple of months. But it was never boring, as my dressing roommate was Richard Dawson, who was one of the funniest people I have ever met.

Bill Holden was very much in love with Africa, and when I told him that my place of birth was Ethiopia, we became friends, and had many dinners together talking about that wild continent, and in particular about his ranch in Kenya. I also told him that Gloria Swanson, his co-star in "Sunset Boulevard," had cut my hair—he said, "You were really courageous!"

One day, as we were in the middle of a shot, David Wolper came and stopped the shooting. He called to me and handed me an urgent telegram: Brigid had given birth to a little girl. She named her Marguerite. The telegram said that she was adorable. Well, I wanted to find out by myself. It was April 26, exactly one year after we were married. Wolper allowed me to spend the weekend in New York to meet my baby daughter. She had Brigid's eyes, thank God, and she was really adorable. I was very proud. I thanked Brigid and returned to Utah.

Later, the rest of the film was shot on location in Italy. The entire cast and crew flew to Rome, where we boarded a bus that took us to our final destination, the charming village of Formia. I could not stop thinking about my two ladies in New York. I called Brigid and asked her to join me for the last days of the shooting. Marguerite was a baby and we did not think that she should be traveling by plane, so Brigid left her with the nanny and came to Italy. I introduced her to Bill, who was very gracious. He really was a distinguished gentleman—educated, worldly, and knowledgeable. At night, we would dine in charming little Italian restaurants, and Brigid and I talked about the future.

That's when we decided to move to LA, where we could raise Marguerite in an environment that was less stressful than the Big Apple.

Bill Holden, Andrew McLaglen, David Wolper, Utah, Italy, Brigid and Marguerite! What else could a man want?

CHAPTER 15

Marguerite

WE WERE now living in LA, and we were enjoying our little house. Marguerite was a year old, and she was growing up to be a very pretty girl. One evening, we were watching TV when a bulletin came on: Robert Kennedy had been assassinated. We stayed up all night watching the news. We were devastated, and felt so powerless. Another tragedy in the Kennedy family. How can anyone still believe that "their" religious God was good? God, or Nature by another name, is good and bad. If God was only good, why would He let great people get assassinated and gangsters like Al Capone get away with murder? If God was only good, and listened to prayers, why would He create wars, hate, earthquakes that destroy churches, tornadoes that kill thousands of innocent people, and recent disasters like HIV, 9/11, Katrina, Harvey, Irma? That's the way Nature is, and no religious God will ever change it. But it is really sad to see that one family can be the target of so much misfortune.

On a different historical level, it was also sad that one year later, Brigid and I started to have marital difficulties. I will not disclose our problems here, because some personal and sensitive matters must remain private, especially when the mother of my child is involved. Let me just say that, because we were still very fond of each other, because we still cared about each other, and we both had Marguerite's best interests at heart, we were able to keep our divorce friendly and amicable.

Every Friday evening, I would pick up Marguerite, and she would spend the weekend with me. It was during one of these weekends that Man landed on the moon. While Walter Cronkite was reporting the event, I taped the whole affair on my little cassette recorder. Marguerite could not understand yet the importance of that event in the history of Mankind, but when I started the recording, I simply said, "Marguerite darling, you are here with me witnessing on live TV, the first steps of a man on the moon. One day, you will understand how extraordinary this is, and you will know that you saw it. So, let's listen to Walter Cronkite." During the taping, Marguerite kept babbling some baby talk. I kept the cassette for several years, and when Marguerite turned 16, I gave it to her. She laughed when she heard herself twaddling!

I was working in different locations, singing from city to city, but I always found time to see Marguerite during the fantasy world of the Christmas season, or during the amusing world of the summer holidays. Her grandmother, Maggie Daly, was happy to see Marguerite close to me because, in spite of the divorce, Maggie and I had remained close. When Marguerite was about three years old, I loved buying her little dresses. Dresses for little girls are so lovely. One Sunday morning, I had taken her for breakfast in the old Schwab's Pharmacy, which was located on Sunset Boulevard. Schwab's was the place where, legend has it, Lana Turner was discovered while she was sitting at the counter, sipping a chocolate malt. Of course, since Marguerite loved chocolate, I would always order a chocolate malt for her. That Sunday morning, she was wearing an adorable little dress and she looked very pretty. After breakfast, we left Schwab's, and as we were walking on the sidewalk, two older gentlemen were coming in the opposite direction. One of them spotted Marguerite and stopped. His eyes were looking at her in disbelief. He said to her, "My God, you are so beautiful! I want to thank you for being so pretty, so here is... " and out of his pocket he handed her... "a quarter !" And little Marguerite took the quarter, smiled and said, "Thank you." It was very touching.

Sometimes, I'd take her with me when I was singing on cruise ships, and I would bring her on stage at the end of my show to introduce her to the audience. She was always a big hit! One trip was during the filming of a mini-series titled "The French Atlantic Affair," which was shot aboard a Carnival Cruise ship. The stars of the movie, Telly Savalas, Shelley Winters, Louis Jourdan—and Stella Stevens in particular—fell in love with her.

I tried to teach her what I had learned in my Jesuit boarding school. In subtle ways, through funny anecdotes or through

On a cruise with my daughter Marguerite, 1978

memories of my adolescence, such as the Père Franchet explanation of God, I was trying to teach her to always concentrate on whatever she had decided to do—whether it was an English composition, a gym exercise, or baking a cake. To make her understand that she should always put 110 percent into any action she chose, and do it well, to the best of her ability, or not do it at all. I asked her to always be honest, especially with herself, and to always, always, always ask questions. I tried to teach her that society has a strong tendency to brainwash people from the moment they are born, to make them believe certain things which are not always factual—such as saying that making love is a horrible sin! I told her that killing people is the worst offense a human being can do, as well as stealing money under false pretenses, like the oil companies and the pharmaceutical conglomerates often do. For mysterious reasons, which are not so mysterious if you take seriously the theory of the book "The Da Vinci Code," religions and certain "Morality Preachers" brainwash us from the beginning of our lives with so called "articles of faith" that persuade us that making love is a terrible sin, but killing people is okay. Has anyone ever asked these "faith masters" why, if lovemaking is a sin, God would have made it so delightful, why He would have made it the source of life and happiness? They make us believe all these things when we are babies, because they know that babies will believe anything without asking questions. Even today, the Motion Picture Association of America will give a PG-13 to a movie in which a gory killing takes place, but an R rating to beautiful and emotional movies that portray a sexual scene—and nobody dies.

Marguerite and I discussed on many occasions the fact that men had invented several religions to take advantage of the mystery of the Creation, and that all the stories she would hear about religions were perpetuated by men, and certainly not by God. Which reminds me of something that a witty gentleman by the name of Richard Fishoff said at a dinner party: "God is a promiscuous real estate broker who promises lands to everyone." It really made me laugh. But I always told Marguerite that when she became an adult, and was able to understand clearly what religions are about, she could choose one, if that's what she wanted. I am glad to report that she never did.

When Marguerite was born, her great-grandmother on Brigid's side flew in from Ireland. She was a staunch Catholic, and I did not want to offend her. So, after several arguments, I compromised, and agreed to have Marguerite baptized, just to please her Irish grandmother. And sometimes, when we were having a little disagreement, I jokingly would tease Marguerite with, "You must be right, you are baptized!" To which she would retort that I was also baptized! True—so I was right, too! But I would pause and say, "Let's think about this for a moment. As I was coming out of the womb, someone told me, even though I could not understand one word, that I was a Catholic, and poured water on my head, even though I did not need a shampoo yet! And nobody asked for my opinion!" Until that philosophy class in Avignon, I really believed that Catholicism was the only religion teaching the true Word of God, not knowing then that in any religion, the Word of God had been written by men, not by God!

I took Marguerite to France to visit my parents a few times. Once, when she was 16 (but looking much more mature), we went to the beach in Nice. The Mediterranean Sea was on her best behavior, calm and warm; the French women lying on the beach were also on their best behavior, calm, warm and topless. The sky was gleaming with the unique hue of blue that you find on the Riviera. On the private beach we had chosen, Marguerite and I were guided to two cushions in the middle of a row of other cushions. She lay down on my right; on my left was an attractive young lady. At some point, Marguerite went for a swim, and I started a flirtatious conversation with the lady on my left. She looked at me with disgust, scolding me for flirting with her while my "girlfriend" was in the water! I tried to explain that she was my daughter—to no avail. When Marguerite came back, I told her that the woman next to me thought that she was my girlfriend. She immediately got a nauseated expression on her face and shrieked, "Ooohhh Noooo"! I asked Marguerite to tell her who I was. She yelled, "He is not my boyfriend, he is *mon père!*" The woman apologized, and told me, "Okay, you can flirt with me now!" For the next Christmas holiday in the U.S., I had a t-shirt made for Marguerite. It read, *He is not my boyfriend* on the front, and *He is my father* on the back. She loved it.

After high school, she applied to Indiana University in Bloomington, and was accepted. I went to visit her a couple of times. It was a beautiful campus, and we liked walking under the dignified trees that had been enjoying their life on these grounds for hundreds of years. They were magnificent. Marguerite was now 18 and very beautiful. She had her mother's eyes. She was quite striking, and I was surprised that she had never mentioned any boy in her life. So I asked her if she had a boyfriend, and she said she was "seeing some guy." I also asked her if she had discovered the joy of lovemaking. She frowned at my remark and said, "Of course not!" Now, I certainly was not trying to encourage her to sleep with all the dummies who would try to take advantage of her, but I explained to her that if she met a nice guy, someone she liked, someone she was attracted to, someone she trusted, there was nothing wrong with experiencing with him the beauty of that natural act created by God. After that conversation, I invited her on a few occasions to come visit me in Los Angeles. Each time, I would tease her with, "So, still a virgin?" And each time, she would ignore me.

One year later, I went to pick her up at the airport, and after the greeting chats, I said, "So, anything new in your love life?" She smiled and whispered, "Yes, you have no more reasons to tease me about my love life. You were right—Nature is terrific!" So we went home, and I opened a bottle of champagne to celebrate. A few days after her return to I.U., she called me to tell me that her girlfriends thought that I was the coolest dad in the world!

Some time later, a new page was turned in our lives. One morning, my phone rang very early. I picked it up: "Allo?... Allo? . . ." All I could hear was someone crying. I kept saying, "Allo... who is this?" Finally, in the middle of heavy tears, a little voice full of anguish said, "Dad... Mom died last night." I was stunned, unable to say a word. When I regained my composure, I said softly, "I am here, my darling... thank you for calling me. I'll come to Chicago to be with you." I jumped on a plane the following day and arrived in Chicago at Maggie's place late in the afternoon. I was still in shock, not understanding how Brigid could die so suddenly, and so young. Maggie told me that Brigid had been sick for quite some time and did not want anyone to know, as she wanted to be remembered the way she had always been: young, healthy and beautiful.

Brigid's death affected me profoundly. Was it because she was the only woman I had ever married? Was it because she was the mother of my only child? Was it because I may still have been subconsciously in love with her? For whatever reason, I could not sleep or eat for many days and nights. She was only 44. I felt terribly guilty for not being closer to her those last few years. I felt the pain for a long time.

Then I thought that I had to get closer to Marguerite, as I was her last parent. Thank God, her grandmother Maggie was still alive, and was taking care of her in Chicago. I must add that when Maggie became very ill, Marguerite in turn, took good care of her, and displayed an admirable devotion to a grandmother who was a special lady.

It was a difficult period in my life with Brigid's passing, and my career slowing down. But when Marguerite graduated from I.U., I went. By some fluke, it was snowing in Bloomington that day... so, they had to transfer the graduation ceremony inside, in the big basketball arena, which was quite exciting, since it was the arena where I.U. had won the NCAA championship two years before. To congratulate Marguerite on her graduation, I wrote the following poem:

Your mother and I, we wanted a child
But we had agreed to wait for a while
          And let our passion play games of the wild.
Your mother and I were not very skilled
In the discipline of mathematics
We miscalculated
The speed of my swimmer
Who reached the egg of life

In a way so discreet
That we did not know it
And when you showed up
You were the cosmic surprise
Of our passion gone astray
And we loved you for it.
When you were a baby,
        Before disposable diapers
I had to change you and clean you
And you knew that I cared for you
        When our life had a change of mind
   Week ends became our only time
        That we spent on merry-go-round
   Watching Armstrong on the moon
        And learning how to build our bond
   And then you grew up very fast
Moving from city to city
From school to high school to college.
But in summer time or Christmas
We'd steal a few days together
Going on cruises or "Star Wars."
And then one day
You felt the pain of your life
When the woman who loved you so
The woman whom we both loved
The one who brought you to this world
The one who made you reach your soul
Took the path to eternity.

But you knew
   That I was there for you
And our bond grew stronger
We lived far from each other
And it was not always easy
To keep alive our affection.
But I will always remember
   What you did for me
   When you were twelve years old.
   We had spent a day
In the Land of Disney
   You loved Mickey so much
   That I bought one for you
And then you held him in your arms
Every day and every night
And he became the center of your life.
The day before Father's Day
   You had to go back to school
At the airport, you kissed me good bye
And said that my Father's Day gift
Was in the closet of my den.
When I came home, I found my gift
The Mouse that you loved so much
The Mickey so close to your heart
Was there with your hand written note:
"Please take good care of him.
It's for you. I love you, Daddy."
That was the purest proof of love

That you could ever give me
   And I want you to remember
      That if I have not always been
         The greatest father in the world
My love for you will always live
   Longer than any other love in my life.
For you are my daughter
And you will always be
My pride.
P.S. Mickey is very old today
   He lives in a suitcase in the attic
      And your note
      Is close to his heart
      And mine.

After the ceremony, I gave Marguerite the poem. She read it, looked at me, and with a crack in her voice said: "I love you, Daddy."

Today, Marguerite is happily married to a gentle man who is also a Gentleman. His name is Joel, and he makes Marguerite very happy. What else can a father ask for? They have given me two beautiful granddaughters, Leah and Hannah. I do not use the word "beautiful," because I am the grandfather, but they happen to be really gorgeous little girls, and I can't wait until we can start discussing what's going on in the world, or what kind of fashionable couture they will favor when they are in their teens, or what kind of food they will enjoy most!

I know that to be interesting, a book must present some serious conflicts. But I cannot remember any serious problems with Marguerite. Many of my friends or acquaintances have children who are lazy in school, or drink, or take drugs, or refuse to make the effort in getting a job; children who believe that everything is due them, children who are troubled, and create grave difficulties for their parents. And some don't even like chocolate! When I see that, I look up to the sky and say, "Whoever you are, whatever you are, wherever you are, I thank you for blessing me with a daughter who has never given me any problems."

Yes, Marguerite makes me very happy, and I am very proud of her.

I am also glad to report that Leah and Hannah love chocolate!

CHAPTER 16

Bette

A

S FAR as my career was concerned, I kept singing in some show rooms like The Eden Roc Hotel and the Doral Hotel in Miami Beach, the Playboy Club in LA and New York, and some other places. I also worked as an actor in several TV shows, such as "The Rockford Files," "Murder She Wrote," "Colombo," "Dallas"—and I even appeared in a couple of films. I kept busy for awhile.

On the WGN-TV station in Chicago, there was a show every Saturday night, called "Continental Café." One season, they were looking for a host with a continental personality, and that's how I was booked to be the MC for that show. We rehearsed during the week, but my Sundays were free. Not far from Chicago, there is a town called Lake Geneva, and the Playboy Club had a beautiful hotel there, with a showroom where different performers were booked to entertain the hotel guests. One day, I received a call from the Playboy Club telling me that a convention of French doctors had made a reservation for a weekend, and asked me if I could do my show for them; I agreed. On the selected Sunday, a limo came to pick me up. When I got into the limo, a couple was sitting there. The gentleman introduced himself as the manager of the lady, who was a singer. He had a club in New York, The Improv, and this lady was the star of the show there. As we talked, I realized that she was extremely funny; I also noticed that she was extremely well-endowed!

By the time we got to the hotel, we had become good friends. That night, she was supposed to open the show with three songs. Not only was she a wonderful singer, but her comments between songs were hysterical. But of course, you had to understand English, and that French audience did not get her jokes, and was not reacting warmly to her. After her second song, the applause were rather tepid, so she left the stage, and said, "These fucking French doctors don't understand a thing, so fuck them, I'm gone!" But I had to do my part, and got a very friendly reception.

Then the three of us had dinner, and enjoyed being together. We even went to her room for a drink and more jokes. Her manager told me that she was going to make a record soon, and could not wait, as he knew that she would make it big. I told them that I was going to sing on a cruise. It was the last trip of an American ship called the Santa Paula from the Grace Line, that would leave from New York for two weeks, going to South America, and back to the Big Apple. I said that I would come to New York with my girlfriend the day before we sailed, and I would love to see them. She said she had a big apartment, and that I was welcome to spend the night there. I accepted, and on the day I arrived in New York, my girlfriend and I went directly to her place. She opened the door and said, "Please come on in, here is your room, refresh yourself, and when you're ready, come join me. I am rehearsing with my piano player."

After we put ourselves together, we went to the room where she was rehearsing, and listened to her beautiful voice. When she stopped, she said, "Hi, Jean-Paul, meet my piano player, Barry Manilow." And she was, of course, Bette Midler!

CHAPTER 17

Sinatra

ONE OF my bookings at the Eden Roc Hotel in Miami Beach
was at the end of January, near my birthday. I was appearing in the Harry's American Bar lounge, an intimate kind of
cabaret. The big star in the main room upstairs was the singer
whom I had admired from the beginning of my career: my idol,
Frank Sinatra! So, in between my three shows, I would sneak
into the main room to listen and learn. It was such a joy to
witness the professionalism of this great performer, who could
have the whole audience in the palm of his hand—not only with
his amazing voice and special phrasing, but also with his unique
sense of humor. I felt so lucky to have the chance to listen every
night to this legendary singer.

One night, just as I was going to start my last show, the manager came to me and asked me to wait a few minutes. "Guess
what? Sinatra is coming to see your show. He'll be here any
minute, so do the best you can. Good luck!" I almost fainted.
Harry's Bar was not a big room, and when I walked on the stage,
I saw that they had sat Sinatra with his entourage four or five
feet in front of me. I had been listening to his records since I
started singing in France; he was, for me, bigger than life. And
suddenly, here he was listening to me! Oh, la, la, I had never
been so nervous, and my mouth became very dry... which does

not help much when you sing! Anyway, I did my show the best I could, and saw Frank applauding me. I could not believe it!

The next day, the hotel concierge handed me a note: "Mister Sinatra has learned that your birthday is tomorrow, and he would like to invite you to a big party that had already been planned tonight for his friends, on the rooftop of the hotel." As you can guess, after my last show, I dressed up and quickly went to the rooftop. At the door, I was welcomed by two very big men who were very friendly, and guided me to a table where a few other people were sitting. Sinatra was not there. One person said to me that they had come with Frank to see my show the night before and that they had enjoyed it very much. I thanked them, ordered a drink, and we chatted.

The room was very crowded, and many couples were dancing to the sound of a fabulous big band. At some point, every couple at the table went to the dance floor, as the big band was playing a beautiful slow dance. Everybody had left the table except for one attractive lady. We started talking, and she said, "Let's go dancing." I agreed, and we were dancing cheek to cheek for about 15 seconds, when a large hand tapped on my shoulder. One of the friendly guys who had welcomed me whispered in my ear, "You can't dance with her, she's Frank's girl." I realized that he must have been one of Frank's bodyguards, and I simply said, "Sorry, I did not know." And ceremoniously, I took the lady back to the table, where we continued talking about everything and nothing. For some unknown reason, Sinatra never came to the table, and I eventually left. That was one of the regrets of my life, that I never had a chance to speak with my idol. But I never forgot the hand on my shoulder!

CHAPTER 18

Los Angeles — Las Vegas — Washington, D.C.

I N LA, there were several syndicated talk shows on TV. One day in 1968, I was booked on The Donald O'Connor Show. In the green room, I met a young lady who was doing public relations for one of her clients, Merrilee Rush, who had a hit record, "Angel in the Morning." She told me that her boyfriend was English, and that he was a rock star in England. We decided to have dinner together. Her name was Charlene Groman, and her boyfriend was Richard Sarstedt, whose brother, Peter Sarstedt, had a number one hit in the US at the time, titled "Where Do You Go To My Lovely." Richard's stage name was Eden Kane, and he had some rock and roll hits in the UK; one of them, "Well I Ask You," was number one. But he wanted to continue his career in America, because that was where all the young singers of my generation wanted to come. We became very close friends, and still are to this day.

When Charlene and Richard decided to get married, an unexpected legal problem sprung up. In order to outwit the problem, they had to have a secret marriage, and Richard asked me to be his best man. So, Charlene, her maid of honor, Richard, and I went to City Hall, wearing big sunglasses so no one would recognize us. Eventually, they said "I do" in front of a judge. A few months later, when everything was cool, they had their traditional wedding with their friends and family. Only four people in the crowd knew that they were already married! Today, they have two grown children: Amy, who is married and has two little boys, and Robby who is a successful chef, and is married to a beautiful French lady, Stephanie; they have an adorable little girl. 47 years later, Charlene and Richard are not only my friends, but they are also "family."

As a single man, I was on the road again... from the Persian Room at the Plaza Hotel in New York City, to the Princess Hotel in Acapulco, Mexico, to the Ritz-Carlton in Chicago... and Las Vegas!

My first show in Vegas was at the Riviera, when Vegas was still that mystic city lost in the desert, that mysterious city of Oz built for gambling wizards, that extravagant playground that pulled neon over your eyes, and where the show-biz legends, the Rat Pack, the movie stars and the gangsters were challenging the stars in the firmament. At "the Riv," there was a closed lounge where Shecky Greene was King. In my humble opinion, Shecky was a genius, one of a kind, a brilliant comedian who did not rely on old jokes, but on his own wit and creativity. I was fortunate to be booked to open his show, which allowed me to enjoy his sparkling humor every night. What a master he was!

My next appearance in that city was in a smaller hotel, the Hacienda, where I was headlining a review called "Turn It On." My opening night was quite successful. Some celebrities had come to see me—among them, Ed Sullivan, Dick Clark and Pamela Mason, whom I had met on a couple of occasions in Los Angeles, and whose British wit I enjoyed very much. It was the most emotional opening night of my career. A couple of years before that night, during the Vietnam War, I had done a benefit for the prisoners of war (POWs) at the Coconut Grove in LA. At the end of the show, a lady gave me a POW bracelet with her husband's name on it: Colonel Raymond Schrump. She asked me to wear it, and I never took it off. We talked for awhile and, to my amazement, I discovered that a few years before, they had been stationed in Dire Dawa for four months! What an unbelievable coincidence!

A few years later, I was watching a television report of the prisoners returning from North Vietnam. As the planes landed, the prisoners came out one by one, and were saying their names in a microphone. When the third plane landed, the first man who came out said, "My name is Colonel Raymond Schrump." I looked at my bracelet and almost fainted. My heart was exploding with joy. I was so happy for Mrs. Schrump, who had told me that she did not know if her husband was dead or alive. I immediately called my manager, and with the help of the Hacienda, we were able to invite Colonel Schrump and his family to my opening night. He was sitting in the front row, and when the show ended, I introduced him. The cheering audience jumped to its feet, and the applause went on forever. With tears streaming down my cheeks, I took the bracelet from my wrist, leaned forward and gave it to him. It was a spine-tingling experience that still gives me goose bumps when I think of it. It was one of the most touching episodes of my life.

After the show, I went to my dressing room to relax, wash my face and change my clothes. As I was buttoning up my shirt, someone knocked on the door. It was Pamela Mason with a very elegant young man. She said, "This is my son Morgan, who just flew back from London. I asked him to accompany me to your premiere."

Both of them were very complimentary, and as they were leaving, I asked Morgan if he wanted to come with me watch a late show somewhere; he accepted. I had a date with one of the girls from the show, "Bare Touch of Vegas," at the Dunes. Morgan was elegant, good looking, and very different from all the other men on the strip, and I knew that the girls of "Bare Touch" would be very happy to "touch" him... and I was right. As they say, what happens in Vegas stays in Vegas!

Morgan was much younger than I, but looked much more mature than his age, and I became sort of his big brother. And like Humphrey Bogart said to Claude Rains at the end of "Casablanca," it was the beginning of a beautiful friendship!

Morgan and I went to Las Vegas quite often. Once, we were early at the airport, and since we had to wait for our flight, we stopped in a bar to get a drink. The place was packed, but surprisingly quiet. As we sat down, it seemed that everybody in the room was looking at us in silence. We looked at each other, wondering if something was wrong with our attire, but everything was fine. After ordering our drinks, we suddenly realized that the people were not looking directly at us; they were staring at the table right in front of us, where a couple was sitting. Looking closely, we saw that the man had no arms. He was smoking, holding the cigarette with his right foot. His left foot was holding his drink. We were astounded. At some point, he put out his cigarette and lit another one, holding the lighter with his left toes and igniting the flame with his right toe. The woman never once tried to help him. We were speechless, lost in amazement. I guess that the man was born without arms, and had been able to develop the incredible ability to use his feet like we use our hands. It was obvious that he knew that everybody was staring at him, and he was enjoying giving a show. Morgan leaned over and whispered to me: "Do you have any idea what his profession is?" I took a pause and said, "Maybe a classical orchestra Conductor?" To which he answered, "I disagree with you. I think that he is a brain surgeon!" It took a big effort on my part not to explode with laughter!

Of course, it was not very nice to make fun of a man who had been able to overcome a tragedy that he must have endured all his life. But as we say in show business, we only make fun of the people we admire. And admiration was not a strong enough word to express the emotion that we felt in front of the prodigious determination of this man who had decided once and for all that having no arms was not important. What a lesson in positive thinking!

After that episode, we resumed our trip to Vegas. It was during these trips that, thanks to Morgan, I had the pleasure of meeting some great stars: Milton Berle (who was really hysterical), Debbie Reynolds (whose talent on the stage was incomparable), Zsa Zsa Gabor (who spoke perfect French), and Jacqueline Bisset (who was then the most beautiful girl in the world).

Morgan and I were big LA Lakers fans, and it was always a treat to go to the Forum, which was then the home of the Lakers team. We saw one game that we would never forget, with Magic Johnson, Kareem Abdul Jabbar, Gail Goodrich, James Worthy and Michael Cooper. It was one of the NBA Finals games against the Celtics: Larry Bird, Kevin McHale, Robert Parish, Dennis Johnson and Danny Ainge. These players were all extraordinary, and it was really a "Show Time" that we enjoyed tremendously. Morgan always teased me when I would strongly disagree with the referee, and scream from the bottom of my lungs with my French accent, "Booooooll Sheeeet!"

Years later, Morgan—who was not a Republican—became involved by accident in Ronald Reagan's campaign for the Presidency, and asked me to help him. When Reagan became President, Morgan was named Special Assistant to the President. I went to Washington, DC, and we spent two glorious years there, enjoying the perks of working for the White House. The GOP was then still a decent Party that respected the Constitution and the rules of justice. Today, the GOP has proven that it no longer respects the wisdom of our Founding Fathers, or their rulings, such as the separation of church and state, and the freedom of speech. Personally, I am very disillusioned with the American political landscape. Politicians cannot be trusted, and that's why I am no longer involved in politics, even though I lean toward the Democrats who are more compassionate. And of course, I can't wait until we get a woman President!

While we were there, the journalists often tried to get interviews with Morgan, whose parents were the famous English actors, James and Pamela Mason. That's how he got to meet Ben Bradlee, the renowned editor of the Washington Post, who dared to risk publishing the story of the Watergate scandal, which was researched and written by Bob Woodward and Carl Bernstein.

We had a beautiful four-story house in Arlington, Virginia; the top floor was Morgan's, the middle one was the living area, and I had the third floor down. Under my floor was another room, with a large Jacuzzi and a picture window that looked on the woods behind the house. In winter, it was delightful to soak in the hot water and watch the snow falling gracefully in the silence of the night, silence that was often broken by the laughter of our various female guests.

One day, Morgan invited Ben Bradlee to dinner with a couple of other guests. Our maid, with my help, cooked a delicious meal. Mr. Bradlee was a very intelligent man and a political encyclopedia. We spent the evening making fun of a lot of politicians, drinking good wines, and listening to Sinatra, Peggy Lee, Dean Martin, and Nat King Cole, whose records were playing in the background. After they left, we thought that they had really enjoyed the evening. The next day, we learned that Mr. Bradlee had told someone we knew that he had had a good time, but that it was such a pity that Morgan and I were gay! I guess that, just because we were living in the same house, he thought that we were sleeping together!

Ah, if he had only known what really happened on those four floors!

Another time, my friend from school, Jean-Louis, came to Washington for a dentists' convention. Morgan was able to organize a lunch in the White House mess, which was run by the Navy. It happened that President Reagan was sitting at a table not far from ours. Jean-Louis could not get over it. He was so impressed that he said to me, "I envy you. All day long, I have to look at bad teeth and smelly mouths, but you really have an exciting life. Yes, I envy you." Coming from my very wealthy friend, I was startled. But it proved to me that money is not always what makes people happy.

Morgan (who loves to travel around the world), lived for several years in the South of France with his beautiful wife Belinda Carlisle, but they recently decided to live in Bangkok.

To each his own, as they say! Their son James lives in West Hollywood. Morgan and Belinda come to visit him once in a while, and that's when we get to see each other. I admire Morgan a lot; he will always be my younger brother.

CHAPTER 19

On the Road

WHILE I was on the road, I met some women, but my schedule did not allow for any serious relationships. Although I was working regularly, my career was not progressing as I had hoped. I could not understand why, but nothing important was happening. In fact, the traditional nightclubs started to close everywhere, and I eventually found myself in a precarious situation. But I kept trying. Some hotels still had rooms with dining and dancing, but they booked what were called "self-contained" groups, meaning that I had to bring my own musicians, my own sound system, and even my own lighting. I was used to the big nightclubs that provided musicians, sound, lighting and professional engineers in charge of the stage. On top of that, by the time I paid the musicians and the rental for the equipment, I did not have very much money left for myself. But I had to go on. So, for about two years, I played those clubs and found out what "paying my dues" really meant!

I try to forget that period, but one funny story is worth telling.

The group and I were relaxing in LA for Christmas. Our next gig was set for New Year's Eve in Edmonton, Canada. We had to open the show on the weekend before New Year's Eve, so the six of us left LA on Christmas Day in two cars and the van carrying our equipment. Our first stop was Vancouver; it took us a day and a half to get there, under a tenebrous grey sky that gave birth to a torrential rain. We arrived in Vancouver around 10 p.m., and spent the night in a hotel. The next morning, miraculously, the sky was clear and the sun was smiling again, even though the temperature was around the freezing point. We left Vancouver and drove for a while in the middle of an enchanting farmland which was very well-tended. On the horizon, the Rocky Mountains were very much alive under their snowy fur coat. We kept traveling, while listening on the car radio to Nat King Cole, Frank Sinatra, Rosemary Clooney, Ella Fitzgerald, Andy Williams, Dean Martin, and many other stars singing Christmas songs. We were laughing, and really were in the Christmas spirit.

Eventually, the road started to climb toward the summit, and patches of snow started to appear. The road was still clear, as the snowplows had done their job well. We had to go over the Rockies during the night, and thought that a little rest and some food would be welcome before the assault on the difficult pass ahead of us. That pass went through Jasper National Park, and would take us to the other side of the mountain. Just six miles before the pass, we found a charming little town with an attractive coffee shop, and we decided to stop there for a couple of hours to replenish our strength. It was a cute town, and full of Christmas frenzy. The snow was falling again. The waiters and waitresses in the coffee shop were very hospitable, and very interested in the fact that we were singers and musicians going to perform in Edmonton for New Year's Eve. Before we left, they told us that the pass should not be a problem, as snowplows were working through the night. Then they wished us good luck, and helped us with the food we got for the rest of the trip.

Around 6 p.m., we filled up the cars at the only gas station still open, and we left. The night was very dark, and the snow was coming down heavily. At the entrance to the park, we had to stop to buy a permit from a guard who was standing in his little cabin. A lamp above the cabin was swinging in the wind, shedding some gloomy light. Suddenly, we had that uneasy feeling that we were in one of those *"films noirs,"* where the lamp keeps swinging above the killer and we can only see half of his face! I went to the guard and I bought the permits. But he said that the plows had not yet arrived on this side of the pass, and that it was mandatory to put chains on our back tires. I had a pair of chains in the trunk. Have you ever had to put chains on your tires? It's not very easy. I tried, and I tried, and I tried... in vain. The musicians in the two other vehicles had succeeded, and they came to help me. It was just impossible. My guitar player, who was quite knowledgeable about those types of things, told me, "These chains are not the right size. They will never fit your tires." I was very upset. I gathered those damn chains, threw them in the trunk, and with an angry gesture snapped the trunk shut. I spoke to the guard, who said that he would not let me go without chains. I told my guys to go ahead, and I stayed in my car with the girl singer, Linda, trying to find a solution. I decided to go back to the gas station to see if they had the right chains.

I was ready to start the car, but the keys were not in the ignition. I asked Linda what she had done with the keys. She said that I had taken them to open the trunk. In those days, there were no inside button to open the trunk; the only way to open it was with the key. The enormity of the problem hit me in the face: I must have left the keys in the trunk when I slammed it shut. Now, there was no way to open the trunk, no way to get the keys, no way to start the car. I panicked for a couple of minutes. Then I composed myself, told Linda to wait in the car. I went outside in the bitter cold, on the other side of the road, hoping that a car might come in the direction of the town. It was close to midnight, and the snow was now above my ankles. That's when my luck decided to wake up from her long sleep! Against all odds, a beautiful Lincoln Continental showed up and stopped for me. I explained to the gentleman driver what my problem was, and he said "get in." He took me to the gas station, and I thanked him profusely. He was the Good Samaritan who really saved me that night. He left, and I told my story again to the young attendant who was ready to close the station. He had the right chains, but he could not leave the station to take me back to my car. I asked him if he knew a locksmith who could open the trunk. He didn't, but he made several phone calls, and finally found someone. I asked him if he could wait a little longer, as it would be easier to bring my car back so he could install the chains himself in the safety of the warm station. He agreed. Now, we were waiting for the person who would open my trunk.

Twenty minutes later, an old car that had seen better days arrived. A man got out of the car with a big smile. His warm and down-to-earth face had fought the wind, the sun and the years. Deep wrinkles were digging his skin and gave him a natural manly look. He introduced himself: "Hi, my name is Dan. I was in the middle of a poker game, and your call helped me lose less money. So, I thank you." We shook hands and we were on our way. In the car, he told me that locks and keys were his passion, and that he had an extensive collection of the most exotic locks. I explained my problem, and he said, "Don't worry, we'll open your trunk in no time. What is the key code for your car?" I said, "The key code?" He said, "Yes, every car has a key code so the keys can be replaced when they are lost." I told him that I was very sorry but I had no idea what my key code was. He said, "Don't worry; in every American car, the key code is engraved on the cylinder of the lock of the glove compartment, so we'll have to get to that cylinder, and we'll make your key." He was a very positive gentleman, and he made me feel very comfortable.

When we reached my car, we found Linda in a frozen state. Since the engine was not running, there was no heat in the car, and she had covered herself with her warmest clothes and the two blankets we had brought with us. She was really happy to see us. Dan had to pick the lock of the glove compartment in order to retrieve the cylinder and get the code key. He sat on the passenger seat and asked me to aim the flashlight on the lock. Picture the scene: I was standing there holding the flashlight, Linda was behind me holding an umbrella, the snow was falling relentlessly, the lamp above was swinging in the wind, the guard in the cabin could not care less, and I was wondering if we would get to Edmonton on time. Suddenly, Dan turned his head to me and said, "I got Sherlock, he is going to give us the secret number!" He took a little machine out of his car, installed it on the roof, worked with it for a couple of minutes, made a key, rushed to the trunk of my car and said, "Open Sesame!" And slowly but surely, the trunk opened, and we all screamed with joy. My car keys were right there on top of the luggage. What a relief! I thanked Dan and offered to pay him, but he refused. He shook my hand warmly, gave a kiss to Linda, and disappeared in the snow. I will never forget him.

We drove back to the gas station where the young attendant was still waiting. He put the chains on the tires, I paid him with a generous tip, and we left around one in the morning. We made it on time to Edmonton, opened the show, and spent there two wonderful weeks—if 30 below can be called wonderful!

CHAPTER 20

The Sensuous Man

M Y MANAGER called me one day: "Dick Clark wants to meet with you, and we have an appointment with him tomorrow." I was not a rock and roll singer, so I wondered what he wanted from me. I went to his office, and there in front of me was the famous Dick Clark, who turned out to be a very kind and charming gentleman. He explained that he had obtained the rights to the book "A Sensuous Man," and that he was going to produce a TV show called "The Sensuous Man" with the backing of the Paramount Studios. His associate on this project was Alan Hamel, who had booked me a year earlier in a variety show that he was producing in Montreal, Canada. They had seen me perform at the Playboy Club, and thought it was natural that a Frenchman played that part. So, after a few auditions and trials, I got the part. Of course, the show was kind of a spoof on the so-called sensuality, and the writer, Kenny Shapiro, wrote some hysterical episodes.

The concept was simple: I was all alone, speaking to the camera, preaching the virtues of Tantric massage, crystals, sexy foods, meditation, intimate touch, and other salacious subjects, but everything was done tongue-in-cheek, with a great sense of humor. That concept was a little too advanced for its time on TV, but it was daring, and a lot of fun. At the end of every show, I would take a bath in a big bathtub built for two—the idea being that if you wanted to clean yourself, you had to take a shower, but a bath was a completely different affair to experiment with the person you loved. In the show, I took baths in milk, Alka-Seltzer, mud, flowers, olive oil, oatmeal, bubbly perfumes and God knows what else! We shot each episode in Montreal.

It was the early 1970s, a time of sexual discovery in America, and that's when Playgirl Magazine began to be published. Alan thought it would be good publicity for the show for me to be one of the centerfolds. Only three or four issues had been published at that time, featuring centerfolds with George Maharis and Fabian, who were big stars then. Even though their private parts were strategically hidden, I thought it was in bad taste, and that it would not be good for my image. I refused, but Alan kept gently insisting. I tried to use the ultimate argument: "The only way I would do it is, if I show everything!" I was thinking that, in this puritanical country, the publishers would not dare to show a man completely nude. Alan spoke with them and, to my consternation, they agreed—I was caught in my own trap!

Since I had appeared at the Riviera in Vegas, plans were made for a shoot in the main showroom, in the afternoon, when the place is empty. We flew to Vegas one morning, and after lunch we went to one of the dressing rooms. I needed some courage, so we smoked a joint. I took off my clothes, and the photographer went into the empty room. I was in the wings with my party, joking and being silly. The curtains opened, and the lights set the stage ablaze. Stage lights are quite strong in these showrooms, blinding the performers. I could not see a thing, but I knew that the photographer was there. All I was wearing was a straw hat and a cane... period. I was kind of dizzy, and I kept moving around the stage while the camera was flashing from the audience. We were all laughing like crazy, and after about 15 minutes, I said "Okay, that's enough, I believe that we have enough pictures by now." The photographer agreed, and the stage lights were turned off. That's when I was able to see the room, and suddenly realized that it was not empty—all the waiters and waitresses were very quietly setting the tables for the first show of the evening. I could not believe it! Totally embarrassed, I ran off the stage, and the staff in the room started to applaud! Alan handed me a towel that I wrapped around my waist, and I returned on the stage to take a bow. The applause and the cheers were deafening... they sounded very loud, I guess, because I was stoned!

It was not a very noble episode, but I thought that you, the reader, would get a giggle out of it. So, now you know that in the sixth issue of Playgirl, I was the first centerfold to show everything. I always joke that the issue should have come with a magnifying glass!

When we were not shooting "The Sensuous Man" in Montreal, I was working on the script in Los Angeles, with Alan and Kenny. But during the weekends, I just wanted to have fun. Every Sunday, Julann Griffin, Merv Griffin's ex-wife, with whom I had kept a friendly relationship, had a tennis party at her house. Her guests were Mel Brooks and Ann Bancroft, Gene Wilder with his then girlfriend Teri Garr, Dick Van Patten and his wife Pat, with their two sons who were terrific players, and a young actress who had just made a commercial with Joe Namath. That commercial brought her to the attention of the Hollywood bosses, but she was still unknown by the public at large. She was then married to the Six Million Dollar Man, Lee Majors. She was really gorgeous. Her name was Farrah Fawcett.

CHAPTER 21

Farrah

EVERY year in Europe, there is an international song contest on TV, held between all the European countries; it is called the Eurovision. That particular year, 1974, Abba had won the contest with one of their songs, "Waterloo." An Italian song titled "Si" came in second. It was a beautiful song, sung in Italian and French by Gigliola Cinquetti. My parents, as they did every year, sent me the French version of the record. Each time I played it for my American friends, they wanted to know the meaning of the lyrics. The song was structured in such a way that between each line I had the time to give them the translation. And they loved it. So, it gave me the idea of recording the song with me singing the French version, and a woman's voice whispering the English translation between each line. One Sunday, I asked Farrah if she would like to record the song with me. She listened to it, enjoyed the English translation that I had written from the French version, and said "Yes." Now, I had to find a sponsor, an arranger, and a way to record the song that I had retitled "You."

A week later, I had a booking at the famous Persian Room in New York's Plaza Hotel. It was one of the last nightclubs where all the big stars had appeared through the years. I had spent several evenings there when I first arrived in New York, and had the pleasure of listening to Carol Channing, Steve Lawrence and Eydie Gormé, Gordon MacRae, and a few other renowned performers, so I was honored to be booked in that legendary music sanctuary. The orchestra was terrific, the sound and lighting very professional, and everybody liked the fact that my charts were well written, my lighting directions were very precise, and that I was not an obnoxious performer!

On opening night, the room was full, and the audience was cheering me with their applause. I was thrilled. Once in my dressing room, a waiter gave me a note from a gentleman named Frank Lieberman, offering me a drink at their table. I accepted, and met two couples who had really enjoyed my show. Mr. Lieberman asked me right away if there was anything they could do for me, in terms of recording some of my material. I was no longer with Columbia Records, and I told him about my idea for the song from the Eurovision Song Contest. I also told him that I had a young girlfriend who was an actress, she was willing to be the American voice, and he might have seen her on the commercial with Joe Namath. Of course, he had seen her, and thought that she was very beautiful. So, we decided to get an arranger, a studio, and we flew Farrah in to do the recording with me. And that's how we recorded the single with the French lyrics written in France, and Farrah whispering my translation of that French version. It turned out to be a wonderful and very sexy record.

At that time, Farrah was not yet very well-known. I remember that, when we entered the studio, she was so shy that she kept holding my hand and place her head on my shoulder. She had never been in a recording studio, and she was very nervous. But I stayed next to her and helped her with the phrasing. And when the recording was over, she hugged me and gave me a big kiss. She was really happy. And so was I!

Now that we had a single (as we called them in those days) to sell, we needed a distributor. I was on the road, and Mr. Lieberman was working on it. It took him about three months to make a deal with an independent record company, NB Records, and the 45 was ready to be released. But we did not know that during that time, Farrah had posed for a very sexy poster in the centerfold of Cosmopolitan, and had been signed to star in a television series. When the poster came out, Farrah became an instant household name. The TV show was "Charlie's Angels"—and you know what happened then! Farrah became a very big star.

But what about our record? I was appearing in Chicago when I received a call from Mr. Lieberman. Farrah's manager threatened to sue him big time if the record was released. Her manager had no part of the recording deal, and he did not want the record to come out. We had a contract with Farrah, and we hired an attorney. But to make a long story short, we did not have enough money to fight that battle, and the record was never released. I tried to call Farrah a few times, but her assistant kept repeating that she was busy. I left a few messages, but she never returned my calls. I guess that she was under pressure to avoid me, and she had to comply with her producers in order to protect her career. Sometimes in Hollywood, fame and money are stronger than friendship. So, now you know how I lost Farrah Fawcett's friendship. That episode broke my heart for some time, but I listened to Sinatra sing "Pick Yourself Up," and I looked forward.

CHAPTER 22

Things Are Changing

I WAS NOT getting any younger. There were no more cabarets, no more nightclubs, no more variety shows... and, unless you had a hit record to perform in giant arenas, singing was no longer an option for singers like me.

That's when I received a telephone call from a post-production studio, asking me if I would be interested in dubbing into French the voice of an American actor in a movie. I went to the studio and dubbed that character. Unfortunately, the translator had translated the dialog word for word, and the lip movements of the American actor I was dubbing were completely out of sync—in general, French takes more words than English to say the same thing. It reminded me of the Japanese movies we used to see on TV, where the English voice started and ended before or after the Japanese actor was opening his mouth! It had become quite a joke in the industry. So, in order to do a decent job of dubbing, I started to make the necessary corrections right there in the studio. I did several dubbing jobs, and each time, I had to make the changes that helped the look of the French version. Then it occurred to me that, since I had to rewrite most of the French dialog, I should be paid as an actor and as a writer. So I asked the person in charge to let me adapt the next film and pay me as a translator/adapter. That's how I started to write the French dialog of some American movies played on the airplanes, where passengers can choose to watch a film in their own language. These French versions were also used on the videos of that particular movie. Then a new technology jumped in, and the era of the DVD began. You must have noticed that, on the starting menu of a DVD, you can choose the language you want to listen to. It became an important business, and I decided to start my own company, Côte d'Azur Productions. I was now producing and directing the French tracks of the American films released on DVDs and for the airlines. I put together a team of French actors living in Hollywood, and they became very good at it. I can say, without bragging at all, that our dubbings are as good as the ones made in France. Of course, all the blockbusters distributed in France must be dubbed in France; it's the law. But not all American movies are distributed in France, so we produce the ones that are released in the States on DVD. It is challenging work, but I really love it.

You may ask what has happened to my singing. Well, in spite of the fact that there are still people who love my style of music, there are no venues in which I can perform. Therefore, I have stopped singing, even though I dream of recording a CD with the beautiful songs of my youth.

Producing those dubbing tracks and doing some voice-over work allowed me to survive quite well. Of course, there were beautiful ladies coming in and out of my life, but, for whatever reason, they did not become serious relationships... we just had a really good time.

At this point, my parents were still alive and had retired in Nice, France, in our little apartment. I went to visit them every year; it was difficult to see them age in front of my eyes. The wonderful mother and father of my youth were now tired and had lost that *joie de vivre* I was raised with. One summer, my father had broken his hip, and my mother and I visited him in the hospital every day. The operation had not been completely successful, and he was scared of not being able to walk ever again.

That's when my mother told me that her last medical check-up had revealed she had leukemia. She was under strict supervision, and had to go through sessions of radiation. My beautiful mother was losing her hair and was quite depressed. I tried to cheer her up, telling her that hair always grows back, and that the only important thing was the beauty of her soul. I reminded her of our times together in Beirut, Djibouti, Harar, Sault. I took her to some famous restaurants, told her a few jokes, and I got her to laugh.

I had to go back to LA, and I kept calling her every day. But that ailment from hell had taken hold of her; she was given one year, maybe two. Everything went very fast. I traveled to her side many times in that year, and at some point, she seemed to stabilize... but not for long. She lost the power of speech, her lips moved slowly, no sound was coming through—but her eyes never stopped telling me "I love you." Every time I went back to LA, I felt that I was losing her, slowly but surely.

Late in October, my telephone rang. The doctor told me, "Condition critical, one day, or two, at best." I ran on the wings of the wind, and at dawn, I was there. I kept her hand in mine, and I looked in her eyes. She saw me. Love burst out of her. A smile came on her face and she said, "I was waiting for you." And as I kissed her, she found the strength to whisper in my ear, "Popaul." It was her last breath.

And I cried.

My father's fear was real: he never again was able to walk on his own. Since he was all alone now, I hired a nurse to go every day to take care of him. But when she arrived in the morning, she found him many times lying down on the floor of the apartment. He would try to go to the bathroom during the night and would fall, unable to get up. With my friend Jean-Louis, we decided to find a place where he could be attended properly. Jean-Louis was able to get him into a special hospital where people in my father's condition were well taken care of. The hospital's name was Les Sources, and it was quite difficult to find a space there. Thanks to Jean-Louis' connections, Les Sources accepted my father. He had his own room, his own TV, and his own telephone. A doctor and several nurses looked after him very well. He was in good hands. My mind was at ease and I visited him a couple of times each year. He stayed there for 14 long years.

The last two or three years, he lost the strength to pick up the telephone and the TV remote. He could barely recognize me. He could not speak intelligible sentences. He could not stop repeating the same words, and always forgot what I had told him a minute ago. It was a very depressing situation.

The last time I was with him was the first week in July. I was talking to him, not knowing if he could understand me, his eyes lost in another dimension. I went back to LA, and on July 14th, Bastille Day, his doctor called me. My father had passed away during the night. I felt a sharp pain. I felt lost, lonely. My father, the man who had sacrificed some of his life to give me a good education, the man who taught me how to fish, the man who convinced me to stand up for what I believe in, the man who asked me to always respect and love women, was gone. It was expected, and I was sad... but I had to smile, because he had chosen to leave on Bastille Day, with the sounds of the fireworks around him. That was like my father, he had to go with a bang! He was 95. I found comfort in the thought that he was now with my mother somewhere in the Universe.

CHAPTER 23

Suzie

IN SPITE of some dark moments, I always embraced life with enthusiasm. I was now at retirement age, and I was comfortable financially. Also, Nature blessed me with good health and a bundle of hair that just refused to turn grey. My "grey" friends were convinced that I died my hair, but I can swear on Marguerite's head that I do not. It is just one of those things... or maybe it is the genes of my father, who never lost his hair and only turned grey in his seventies. I even lost movie roles for people my age because I did not look old enough! Anyway, life was treating me fairly—except in the domain of a long-term liaison. I was losing hope of finding someone to share the rest of my existence with, and I had accepted the fact that I never would.

My friends Charlene and Richard, whose "secret" marriage I had attended, give big parties for their birthdays every year, to which I am always invited. Their many friends are there; I would see the same people every year, and became friendly with some of them. One year, a very pretty brunette attracted my attention. I thought she was someone new, and asked Charlene to introduce me. Charlene told me that I should see a doctor to check my memory cells, because she was actor Yale Summers' wife, her name was Suzie, and I had met them before. Then, I remembered. They were a charming couple. I had been coming to these parties with a different date every year, and Suzie and Yale always teased me with, "Is she THE one?" The following years, I always enjoyed chatting with them. But, even though I found Suzie quite attractive, I always kept my distance because she was married, and I respected her husband, who was very bright and nice to me. I never socialized with them, except at those parties. I did not know them very well, but I really liked them.

One year, on Richard's birthday, Charlene had given a dinner in a restaurant where everyone was sitting around a large table. Suzie and I were seated next to each other. We talked about life in general, and at some point, I asked her where Yale was. She answered, "I don't really know, but I guess he is at his home." I could not understand, and I said, "What do you mean HIS home?" She said, "We have been separated for about eight years, but we are very friendly, and we usually come together to these parties, even though we no longer live together. But this year, he could not make it."

I was very surprised by this revelation and I said that I was sorry. But right in front of me was that pretty lady with a starry night in her hair, a face in white satin, a bright twilight in her eyes, and a smile that would have made Mona Lisa jealous. She had a great sense of humor, the way I like it, and she was oozing feminine gentleness, the way I love it. I looked at her, wondering if she was seeing someone else. I thought to myself, life is short, and I am not getting any younger. Without any hesitation, I said, "Would you like to have dinner with me?" That question took her by surprise, and she waited a moment before answering. "I am having dinner with you right now." I said, "How about another night?" She said, "I have to think about it." It made sense, since she really did not know me very well. We spent the rest of the evening enjoying the food, chatting about the people we knew in our business, and discovering that our politics were very similar. Toward the end of the evening, I asked her again if she would have dinner with me. She gave me her phone number, and asked me to call her a couple of weeks later. She said, "Then, we'll see!"

I called her two days later. We had fun on the phone, and she confessed that she had called Charlene to find out more about me. The report was obviously good, because she accepted a date for dinner.

We had several dates, and started to introduce each other to our friends. All my friends thought she was terrific; they exhorted me not to be an idiot and do something stupid that could turn her off. My friends had never before expressed such an opinion about my other ladies. Then I met Suzie's children, and that closed the deal! Jordan is married to gorgeous Tia. His stunning sister Jolie (yes that's her real name, and she is "*très jolie*"), is married to Kip. Jordan is a very talented songwriter, and Jolie is a gifted actress. I liked them all right away, and we got along very well. Suzie and I started to see each other quite often, and one day, I asked her if she would like to come with me to Chicago, where I was going to visit my daughter Marguerite, her husband Joel, and my granddaughters Leah and Hannah. She said yes, and we flew together. It was a great success. Marguerite and Joel liked her a lot, and the little girls could not leave her alone! That's when I started to realize that, the more I knew Suzie, the more I liked her, to a point where I fell in love with her.

Life is really unpredictable. I thought that I would never

fall in love again, and there I was, falling back to my passionate youth! It was a new and exciting episode in my life, and I felt like I was 20 again!

Suzie is a unique female who possesses all the qualities I am looking for in a woman: she always has kind words for people, she knows how to exude tenderness towards me, she always startles me with her good common sense, she always cracks me up with her wit, she never locks horns with me when we disagree, but very calmly explains why she is right, and above all, she is a good cook and a good lover. And she also did a great job in raising two bright and charming children. So, when I look at myself in the mirror, I say, "What a lucky bozo you are!"

I took her to the Provence of my childhood, the Provence which is still not invaded by a lot of tourists, the Provence where the Cigales are still not afraid to sing their songs of love during the transparent summer nights. I took her to my little village of Sault, where we went to visit the new owners of my grandmother's lavender farm, a gem in the middle of glorious purple and green fields. I took her to the luscious restaurants hidden in the heart of that blessed land, and to the Moulin de Daudet, the windmill where the famous French poet Alphonse Daudet wrote his delightful books. I showed her the Pont du Gard, built by the Romans before Christ, an amazing architectural marvel that has resisted the assault of the elements and the aggravations of the centuries, yes, they don't build them like that any more. I took her to the original restaurant, La Chaumière, where they cook everything in the fireplace and ask you what herb you want on your meat or your fish—thyme, rosemary or anything else—and go pick it in their own garden. We went to L'Isle Sur-La-Sorgue, where they have unique antique shows every weekend that attract antique dealers from around the world. And of course, I took her to Saint-Paul-de-Vence, in the heavenly La Colombe d'Or, a little inn which was opened in the mid 1800s by a very smart innkeeper who would give a free and friendly roof to some young artists who were broke. He would feed them and only ask for a painting in return. That's why today, on the walls of La Colombe d'Or, you can admire the paintings of these penniless young artists whose names were Van Gogh, Miro, Matisse, Rouault, Picasso, and other "unknowns!"

Then she took me to her paradise, Hawaii. Every evening, we would walk to the beach, hand in hand, enjoying the irresistible scent of the magnolia trees, singing "Some Enchanted Evening," and watching the little birds with their red ties bouncing in front of us. Proudly, she would point to the sky, and like a magician, she would turn its color from emerald to fire, while the sun was melting away behind the horizon. Then, listening to the seductive music of the Hawaiian guitars, we would drink the typical cocktails with the little umbrellas on top. We were lost in wonderland, feeling that just being together was enough.

She also took me to Canada, where her sister Nina lives with her husband David. It's her little nest, where she can relax away from the noise of LA. Vancouver is a charming city, its people are extremely friendly, and it's always a pleasure to spend a few days there.

One day, we decided to fly to another planet, the islands of French Polynesia, also known as Tahiti. We did not go where thousands of tourists spoil the serenity of that paradise. We found some very small islands with wild beaches like the ones you can only see in the travel magazines that make you wonder,

"Where are those places?" Our first island was Kia Ora Sauvage, on the Kia Ora lagoon. There are only five bungalows on Sauvage, no electricity, no TV, nothing... just the quiet breeze in the palm trees, the warm caress of the sun, the peaceful melody of the waves, and of course, the clear blue-green water of the lagoon. We walked around the island in the water that only came up to our knees. In these waters, there is a special species of shark that does not attack people. They measure about four or five feet, and come dancing around you. At first, I was a little nervous and did not dare to go in, but Suzie had been there before, and assured me that I had nothing to fear. So there I was, taking pictures of these beautiful sharks caressing my legs in the shallow and transparent water; it was amazing. The man in charge cooked dishes with only the ingredients found on the island, and he caught fresh fish every day. Healthy and delicious. We were Adam and Eve... except there are no snakes on these islands! It was one of my most romantic experiences.

Our next island was Vahine, with six bungalows on the beach and three bungalows over water. Ours was over water, and was unexpectedly extremely comfortable. The chef was exceptional. On the continent, he could have opened a restaurant with three stars! We shared our lunches and dinners with the other customers, three sophisticated couples, one French, one Swiss, and one Dutch. Like us, they loved the quietness of this faraway land, where we could forget the uproar and the violence of the world. The three Tahitian staffers were adorable. In addition to their regular jobs, one of the guys played the guitar, and our waitress was dancing to it, with sexy Tahitian hip movements.

If you ever wish to go to the end of the world—or, as I said, to another planet—that's it! Everybody is very kind and relaxed.

Even the sharks are friendly, as they were just looking at us in a gentle way. Suzie and I had found Paradise!

Our last island was civilized. Moorea is lovely, and the people are also very nice, but it is kind of crowded with packaged trips tourists, and not as unique as Sauvage and Vahine. We came back home with the knowledge that, if the humans were willing to put aside their egos, their greed, their lies, their dishonesty, and their stupidity, it could be possible to live in a peaceful world. But that's a dream that exists only in the Hollywood movies... or in the Tahitian islands! Bing Crosby, Bob Hope, and Dorothy Lamour made us discover the beauty of the Leeward Islands.

Since day one, Suzie and I have been TOGETHER with capital letters! And now, 13 years later, every morning is the first morning of our love, as well as every night. We travel together, we cook together, we laugh together, we enjoy life more than when we were young. There's something to be said about life after 60!

Suzie, circa 2012

But my experience has taught me that life at any age is worth living. When everything has been said and done, nothing, and I mean nothing, is better than Suzie taking refuge in the nest of my shoulder before we go to sleep, and whispering shamelessly "I love you." It may sound corny to some "hip" people, but at the end of the day, it makes the simple man that I am very happy. Not too many people, even the so-called movers and shakers, can say that. I may not have millions in the bank, but I have real emotional happiness in my heart. Now, I can tell Suzie, "You are THE one!"

CHAPTER 24

Lucy

IT WAS a hot summer in Southern California. While the sun was having fun watching all the earthlings trying to dodge the record temperatures, Suzie and I were keeping cool in our air-conditioned home. I was relaxing in my shorts and T-shirt. The phone rang. I picked it up, and a woman's voice asked for Jean-Paul Vignon. I said, "I am Jean-Paul Vignon." Then, in a shy way. she said, "I am sorry to disturb you. I found your phone number on the Internet, and I do not mean to cause you any problem, but there is something I must tell you, and you will understand why at the end of my story." I listened, and she continued:

"My name is Jennifer and I don't expect you to remember me, but you might recall that in February 1977 you were appearing at the Ritz-Carlton in Chicago." I said, "Yes."

"You played there for a couple of weeks. We went out together a few times, just for the fun of it, nothing serious. Since you were on the road, going from city to city, you left Chicago and we did not keep in touch. At that time, a gentleman who was in love with me asked me to marry him, and I agreed. But I soon realized that I was pregnant, and that you were the only man who could be the father. I told my gentleman that I was pregnant with someone else's baby, without telling him your name. He said that he was going to marry me anyway, and would recognize the child as his own. I never tried to get in touch with you, I did not want to bother you, since I did not even know where you were living. I got married, I gave birth to a beautiful baby girl, and we named her Lucy. To avoid any problem, we did not tell Lucy that my husband was not her biological father. A few years later, we had two more baby girls, and the three of them grew up very close to each other. Sadly, my husband died seven years ago, and it took some time for my daughters and me to overcome that difficult tragedy. I must tell you that Lucy is very different from my two other girls. She is very independent, and loves to travel. Right now, she is in Antarctica working in the NASA base. Everything was fine until this past January, when my two other daughters were going through some of their father's old letters, and found one that he had written to his parents just before he married me. He told them that he was going to marry me, even though I was pregnant with someone else's baby, but that would not stop him, because he loved me a lot. My daughters came to me with the letter, and asked me if it was true. I had to tell them the truth, and they made me promise that I would tell Lucy that her biological father was still alive. Lucy is coming back home at the end of September, and I will have to find the strength to explain to her what really happened. I guess that she will be upset, and I don't know what her reaction will be. The reason for my call is certainly not to ask you for anything, except for one simple thing: in case she would like to contact you, please be nice to her."

Wow—I was flabbergasted! Such a story! I was transported back in time... but the sun in the bright sky was pitching balls of 104 degrees, and brought me back to reality: it was damn hot, it was still summer, and I was still in shorts and T-shirt. As I regained consciousness, I told Jennifer that of course, I would be nice to her... but that before I'd welcome her with open arms, I had to be one hundred per cent sure that I was the father, as I had to break the news to my family and my friends, and I wanted to make sure that I could prove what I was talking about. I asked her to let me know the outcome of her conversation with Lucy, and that when she was ready, I would take care of the DNA test. She agreed, and did not object at all to the test.

I told the story to Suzie, who thought that it was very romantic. She teased me and called me Johnny Appleseed, but she was very excited at the same time, and started making plans about how and when we would be able to go meet Lucy. She really was a good sport! Then I called Marguerite to give her the news. When I finished the story she started to cry. I was surprised, and asked her, "Why are you crying?" She answered, "You mean that I am no longer your only little girl?" I tried to calm her down and cheer her up, but she was not sure how to react. That's when she let me know that she was pregnant again with another little girl—Joel is a fast worker! That was some day: a new daughter *and* a new granddaughter in 104 degrees! Life really is a bowl of chocolate mousse!

Lucy came back to the United States in September. Jennifer spoke with her, then called me. Lucy did not take the news very well, but seemed to like the fact that she had a biological father. She told her mother that she might be willing at some point to get in touch with me, but not yet. So, all I had to do was wait and see if she would ever call.

About a month later, I received a long letter that started with these first words: "Hi Jean-Paul, so it seems that you are my father!" The rest of the missive was very warm and very well-written. She explained what she was doing, and said that I could call her whenever I wished. The letter contained some photos of her in Antarctica and in Alaska, and it was a shock to me to see how much she looked like me when I was her age. I called her and said very simply that I would love to meet her but that we had to go through the formality of the DNA test before we could make any plans. She said that she understood, and that she would do whatever was necessary. I organized an appointment in one lab in Chicago and in one lab here in LA, and then our two specimens went to the lab that would figure out the truth, once and for all.

I was told that I would get the results within a week, but nothing came. One evening, I was in a studio, recording a voice-over project when my cell phone rang. I had forgotten to turn it off in the recording booth, and I was not happy that someone would call me at that inopportune time. I answered the call, "Yes, who is this?" A little voice said, "Jean-Paul? This is Lucy." I answered that I had to call her back because I was working, and she said, "Okay, I received the results and there is a 99.97% chance that you are my father. Call me later," and she hung up!

I was standing there gasping, my mouth opened; I was incapable of saying a word. The producer asked me if I was alright. I told him the news, and asked him for ten minutes of rest. I called Lucy back right away to let her know that I was glad to find out that I had a beautiful 28-year-old daughter, that we would find a way to meet each other, and that I would call her in the morning to continue this conversation. As I was coming back to the microphone, the producer said, "Let's finish so you can give us some cigars!" And that's how I found out for sure that I had a second daughter!

The next morning, I called Lucy again, and we started to learn a little more about each other. At some point, she said her mother had told her that I was a singer, to which she answered, "A singer? Are you sure that he is my father? I cannot sing a note!" I guess that it was the one gene of mine that she had not put into her pocket—the 0.03% that did not show up in the DNA test! Eventually, I asked her when we could meet in Chicago. She said that she was leaving for Honduras the following week and would not come back until the month of March. So, I had to wait until then for us to get together.

Christmas and New Year's Eve were wonderful with Suzie and her family. We were often on the phone with Marguerite, Joel and Leah. The pregnancy was progressing well, and I was keeping them aware of what was happening with Lucy. One day, Marguerite (who has a good sense of humor) said, "You know, Dad, there may be more Lucys around. If I were you, I would no longer answer my telephone!" That really made me laugh! Then we made plans to go to Chicago the first week in March, so I could see Marguerite before she gave birth, and at the same time meet Lucy.

The snow in Chicago had melted away, and even the tulips were showing the tips of their noses. Spring was around the corner. Suzie came with me to Chicago, and we stayed at Marguerite's house. It is true that a pregnant woman radiates a certain glow; Marguerite was beautiful, and was handling her pregnancy very well. It was her second one; now, she knew how to deal with it like a pro!

We made an appointment to meet Lucy in a restaurant, and the next day, Marguerite drove us to the train station on our way to the encounter. Suzie went shopping, and I went to the restaurant by myself. I was standing in front of the desk when the door opened, and there she was. She smiled, put her arms around me, and we embraced. My heart was beating fast, and I am sure that hers was, too. She was very pretty. We had lunch, and talked about many things. I called Suzie to ask her to join us for coffee, she arrived, looked at Lucy and said, "You could have avoided the expense of the DNA test. Just looking at her, I know she is your daughter!"

The next day, we took Lucy's mother and sisters to lunch, and another chapter in my life was beginning. Just a year before, I was an accomplished bachelor with only one daughter and one granddaughter... suddenly, I had two daughters, two granddaughters, and my wonderful Suzie. So many women in my life... I was in heaven!

The following week, Marguerite sent a letter to Lucy to welcome her in the family. And once in a while, Marguerite asks me, "Any more phone calls, Dad?"

CHAPTER 25

Utopia

No, I have not gotten any more phone calls... yet! But after many years in Los Angeles, working in "show business," being able to do what I love doing—performing, acting, singing, lending my voice to replace the voice of American stars in the dubbed French versions of American movies, producing different shows, and fighting for the actors' rights with the Screen Actors Guild—I can say that I have seen everything, even though in this business, there is always something new to see, something new jumping out of the least expected places. But one thing I have not yet seen is the Utopia I thought I would find in Hollywood.

Thomas More's definition of Utopia is an ideal imaginary island nation, which the English philosopher first dreamed of in his 1516 novel. A place of ideal perfection does not, and will never, exist—even though Vahine comes close to it—but it is possible to dream about it. And that's what Hollywood excels at doing. It could also be said that Utopia is an imaginary woman of ideal perfection, but my Suzie comes close to that, too!

Hollywood is a two-faced wonder.

On one hand, you have the world of creativity, where brilliant minds are really able to bring to reality the dreams of the human race. That world is populated by the writers, the directors, the actors, the cameramen, the decorators, and all the people involved in the production of a project. In the beginning, the people who started it all were exceptional creators with a chimerical vision. They knew how to entertain the masses and educate them at the same time. Names like Abel Gance, David O. Selznick, John Ford, Charlie Chaplin, Daryl Zanuck, Joseph Mankiewicz come to mind, and are only a few of the greats who have made us dream in the darkness of the movie theaters, and have brought class to Hollywood. Willingly or unwillingly, they were able to develop our brains, and made us see the light in many social issues. They created mirages in the desert of Southern California, but at the same time, they reminded us that we need water to survive in it. They made classic films. In some ways, they created a form of Utopia.

On the other hand, you have the world of greedy used-car salesmen whose double-talk and hype make promises that fly away like balloons in the sky. They make mediocre movies, and they give a bad name to Hollywood.

Hollywood is not the Utopia that I was trying to discover, because it is not a perfect place. But the Hollywood I like and respect at least tries to invent on the screen a kind of Utopia that the whole world is looking for.

My generation was enthralled by the stars who were bigger than life: James Stewart, Cary Grant, Lana Turner, Gene Tierney, Errol Flynn, Marlene Dietrich, Henry Fonda, Lauren Bacall, Humphrey Bogart, Rita Hayworth, Brigitte Bardot, Sophia Loren, William Holden, and so many others who allowed us to forget for an instant the horrors of World War II, and the injustices of the world.

I hope that the generation of today can appreciate what these people did. But we are lucky to have some worthwhile successors like Steven Spielberg, Jane Fonda, George Clooney, Julia Roberts, Brad Pitt, Angelina Jolie, Michele Pfeiffer, Tom Hanks, Will Smith, Jack Nicholson, Cate Blanchett, Warren Beatty, Halle Berry, and of course Meryl Streep, to mention a few. They keep the dream alive, and we desperately need a good dream these days! Not everyone may be conscious of it, but these people are lifting up our lives by making us believe in our dreams.

That kind of Utopia is enough for me, because life is really wonderful if we know what to do with it. The so-called intellectual people will, without a doubt, find my philosophy simplistic. Yes, it is simplistic, because I believe that life is really simple. Of course, we can make it complicated, and decide to complain about everything. But as far as I am concerned, I look at life right in the eyes, with common sense and honesty, and I don't let myself be intimidated by the politicians or the religious zealots. I ignore and disregard the people who try to complicate everything in order to take advantage of me. I may be a debonair type of guy, but I am very cautious, and I never believe anything unless it can be checked thoroughly. That's why I taught Marguerite to always ask questions, and I hope that she will teach the same lesson to Leah and Hannah. Yes, that philosophy may sound simplistic... but it worked for me, and it's one of the reasons my hair is not completely grey, yet!

I am now enjoying that season of life when the green leaves turn to red and dance one last time with the breeze, before falling on the soil dampened by the night rain; when the sun is still shining, but through a cooler sky; when mushroom heads dare to pierce the ground and parade their true colors; and when life continues to throb, but at a more relaxed pace.

But for me, it still feels like spring. My mother, Brigid, Marguerite, Leah, Hannah, Lucy, and now my beautiful Suzie... I have always been surrounded by women who were exceptional ladies, and I thank Mother Nature, the Goddess of the Universe, for blessing me with such joy.

That's why, in the distant future, when all the leaves have disappeared, when the sun no longer shines, when the mushrooms' heads are frozen under a sheet of sparkling snow, when life no longer throbs, and the time has come to scatter my ashes at sea, I ask my friends and family to smile, and only remember the good times we shared together. Since there will not be a tombstone, I would love to see in the sky a plane pulling a banner that reads, "He Loved Women."

And the guy from Ethiopia will be forever in his Utopia.

ACKNOWLEDGEMENTS

WHEN Suzie and I started dating, we revealed to each other the interesting events of our lives, and she always found my events quite fascinating. She kept telling me that I should write them down. I started writing, and the memories kept pouring out of my brain. That's how I wrote this book. So, my first and unconditional thank you goes to Suzie, who is my Loml (Love of my life). She is not only the reason for this book, she also saved my life... but that's another story!

Of course, I have to thank my editor, Alexandra Leh, who guided me in the right direction. She really was a good teacher and I owe her a lot of "merci beaucoup!"

Then, my public relations lady, Claire Arnaud-Aubour, did not stop encouraging me, and did an elegant job of promoting this book. So, I thank her for her patience and her creativity.

And last but not least, I want to thank my family. First, my parents, who gave me the opportunity to travel this unusual journey, and who raised me to be a gentleman with decent and classic values. Then my gorgeous daughter, Marguerite, and her wonderful husband, Joel, and my two granddaughters, Leah and Hannah, whom I admire profoundly.

What makes me a very happy man is the fact that all the people involved in this project have become very good friends, because they believed in me and in my journey from Ethiopia to Utopia. Thank you from the bottom my heart.

ABOUT THE AUTHOR

J EAN-PAUL VIGNON was born in Ethiopia not long before
World War II, of a French father and an Italian mother. He
spent his childhood in Djibouti, and studied in France. His
exotic background gave him a passion for life, and imbued his
singing style with an irresistible sensuality.

As a boy, Vignon was fascinated by movies. As a teenager,
he admired the great French singer-songwriters Charles Trenet
and Charles Aznavour, and was also attracted to American
singers like Frank Sinatra. Vignon's expansive musical taste
gave his style a uniquely universal appeal.

As a young man, Vignon appeared in Paris cabarets, recorded under his own name, and starred in two French films. When
he sang on Le Liberté *en route* to the United States, he was
offered an opportunity to develop his career in America—the
dream of a lifetime.

In New York, he made his debut at The Blue Angel, opening
the show for a young Woody Allen. Ed Sullivan's scouts saw
him, and signed him for eight appearances. He became a regular
guest on The Merv Griffin Show; his European charm, natural
humor, and special charisma delighted American audiences.
After he moved to Los Angeles, he became an American citizen,
and made his American film debut with William Holden in
THE DEVIL'S BRIGADE. Among his many other acting roles,
Vignon's voice can be heard in such films as SHREK and 500

DAYS OF SUMMER, in which he is the French Narrator. Vignon is a devoted father to Marguerite, and grandfather to Leah and Hannah, and lives very happily with his wife Suzie in Beverly Hills, California.

85701027R00095

Made in the USA
San Bernardino, CA
22 August 2018